The Sanctification Walk

A Devotional Reflection on Allowing God to Set Us Apart for His Work

J. Anthony Offer

The Sanctification Walk

Copyright © 2016 by Joe Anthony Offer

All rights reserved. No part of this book may be reproduced or transmitted in any form or by any means without written permission of the author.

ISBN 978-0-9982100-0-1

Library of Congress Control Number: 2016959721

Published by Kingdom Kaught Publishing LLC
Denton Maryland USA
Printed in the USA

Edited by Sarah Gardner

Cover design by Antonio Palmer

Acknowledgments

I first and foremost want to give God all the glory and honor that is due Him. He is a sovereign and mighty God who does what he wants to include calling a man such as myself to do things that were never imagined before. I owe my all to our heavenly Father. I also want to give the just honor to the woman who gives me my inspiration for life as a whole, while putting up with late night writing and study sessions, early morning prayers, endless meetings and an aggressive ministry schedule, my wife Monique. I also want to acknowledge my children Sami'a, Brenden, Jordan and Tori for their endless love, support and deep well of material for me to meditate on.

In ministry there are several mighty men of God who have helped to teach me, lead me and point me toward God at the most opportune times in my life. First the late Reverend Cleo O. Albury, Jr., Pastor of Bible Missionary Baptist Church in Miami, Florida. He was the wisdom that my dad sat me in front of to be accountable for poor grades and ill behavior. A disciplined man of God sure in the foundation of the Word that he gave me. Reverend Doctor Phillip W. Davis,

Sr., Pastor Emeritus of Inter-Denominational Church of God in Gaithersburg, Maryland; He has been a constant inspiration, mentor and molder of my faith for my entire life. Bishop Paul E. Lee, Pastor of New Bethlehem Freewill Baptist Church in Baltimore, Maryland; who ushered me into church leadership (from minister of music to deacon) and eventually into pastoring. He poured more into me than I thought I could hold. I'm glad he has never seemed happy to let me go. Yet he was happy that God chose me for a work and rejoiced in that great shift. All of these men are responsible for the love I have for the Word, teaching and ministering in it.

I also want to thank some of the men of God that I have met along the way. These men have stood with me in ministry whether it was spreading the Gospel, advocating on behalf of the community or just being an accountability partner. I thank God also for many more who have shown so much support along the way.

I want to thank my church family who has shown me that my work in the Kingdom does make a difference in this world. They let me love them, teach them and stand with them in the good and bad times. They even let me mess up every now and then. Thank you to Harvest Crusade Ministries, Glen Burnie, Maryland. God is not through with any of us yet.

Finally, I must honor those charged with my life development. They have gone on to glory but this book is dedicated to their memory. My Mother, Barbara Offer who despite distance and disability was more of a mother to me than many who were healthy and present. I honor my father, Joe Offer who was the one who put discipline in my heart. My grandfather Edward W. Davis who taught me that life is not complicated if you work hard, have respect and are compassionate. My Grandmother Ellen Nickens who always told me that I would be more than anyone has ever realized or expected. I'm still growing, Nan. And to my last living Grandmother Catherine Davis, who just loves me because she knows I'm crazy. She knows I need one person to love me AND laugh at my craziness.

Table of Contents

Introduction 1

Day 1 What Does Sanctification Mean to the Christian? 5

Day 2 A Solid Foundation 11

Day 3 A Simple Prayer Will Do 19

Day 4 Finding Our Way Out of the Darkness 29

Day 5 Get Out of Your Way! 39

Day 6 Let the Words of My Mouth 49

Day 7 The Attitude Adjustment 59

Day 8 Give it ALL You've Got 71

Day 9 Now Faith Is 79

Day 10 Peace Like a River 91

Day 11 In Whose Kingdom Do You Fit? 101

Day 12 Be Yourself, God Will Do the Rest 111

Day 13 Discernment 121

Day 14 Our Worship Reveals the Depth of Our Relationship 133

Day 15 The Blood, God's Correction Fluid 143

Day 16 You are Called to Action 149

Day 17 Committing to God's Order 153

Day 18 Fearlessly Set Apart 159

Day 19 Live in Your Future 165

Day 20 Caged Birds Long to Fly 173

Day 21 Signed, Sealed, Delivered 181

Introduction

The Sanctification Walk was born out of a burning desire to get in position for God to use me in my purpose according to His will. The Scriptures which call us to be holy as He is holy continued to roll over in my head endlessly. More specifically Leviticus 20:26 says, *"you must be holy because I, the Lord, am holy. I have set you apart from all other people to be my very own."* There are several points that are nestled in this very brief but potent verse. We find an obligation. We find a standard. We find our Lord. Finally, we find our place.

These four things draw a distinction between the children of God and the rest of the world. God doesn't call the world to be holy. They are called to turn away from sin and turn to Him. They can't live up to God's standard because they have not yet assumed the covering of God's mercy through acceptance of salvation. The world's lord is the prince of darkness, Satan. In him there is no light. Lordship of the creator is marked by light and life. Finally when we live in the separation of sin we do not belong to the Kingdom of

The Sanctification Walk

God. I began to realize that my life as a Christian was lacking and wanting of excellence in Him. My good wasn't good enough. The very God that I served had released a fire within me to come into a powerful alignment with His will. No longer was it fashionable in my mind to ignore the source of the grace which had preserved me for so many years. I had made it through several catechisms in my walk into ministry. They were administered from being licensed as a minister to ordination and on to installation as a pastor. In all of the knowledge of God's Word, in all of the levels that He lifted me up, I still had a burning fire within me to reach even higher. I Corinthians 10, explains the heart of those who know through experience as well as faith what God can and will do in their lives. Still there are those that God is not pleased with because in their faith they are still tangled up in the rest of the world. In that group are the Christians who are trying to cover up their short falls by being judgmental toward others. Their lack of mercy and grace is evidence of forgetting they are vulnerable to the same sin as they condemn others for.

The human condition is amusing to me while bringing me to tears on so many other occasions. We are an endless string of one act plays riddled with

Introduction

contradictions and unappealing revelations about our character. On one hand we declare with great enthusiasm our values and great moral convictions. Then on the other hand we act against the very declarations that we made. A tragic comedy if ever there was one. *Alas poor Christian, I knew him well.* We act like we have literally lost our minds. In actuality, we have. The loss happened in the Garden of Eden. Ever since then we have struggled to regain it. But the struggle between flesh and spirit rages on to the point where like me, a fire has to burn within that propels us toward God.

Sin is like gravity working against a spaceship fighting to get out of the atmosphere. Our heart wants to get to a heavenly realm. In order to get there our main rockets have to burn full force driving us upward. A spaceship has a guidance system, a preset path to journey through as it races from the pull of earth's gravity. The engineers that designed the rockets have studied the science that determines just how much thrust is necessary to break free of the gravitational pull of the earth. Armed with that information they built rockets powerful enough to overcome the gravity. The thrust is stronger than the forces that want to hold the rocket captive. So it is with us. The power of the Holy Spirit is far greater than the pull of sin. God has made a way for us to overcome that which keeps us from God's Presence and our potential in Him as He inspired His writer in the Bible to say, "Greater is He that is in me than he that is in the world" (I John 4:4).

If you too have a longing for lasting and sustainable growth in your walk with God then this is the book for you. It is time to take the burning embers within you and place them under the breath of the Lord blowing ever so gently on them until they become a raging inferno of passionate worship.

HOW TO GET THE MOST OUT OF THIS BOOK

This was originally written as a 21 day devotional meant to usher the reader into the presence of the Lord over the course of three weeks. This would build habits of sanctification in the reader. To get the same benefit out of this book I suggest that you read one chapter a day and meditate on it as you pray and fast as the Lord will lead you. At the end of each chapter is a prayer. Read the prayer out loud as it will minister to you to hear it. As you speak it will also become a declaration in your spirit. Enjoy your journey and may God pour His Spirit out on you in these 21 days.

Day 1

What Does Sanctification Mean to the Christian?

It is important to make sure that terminology is clear when discussing a topic. As we begin the 21 days of the "Sanctification Walk," we need to understand beyond the notion of developing habits to live the way God wants us to live. That is actually the means to reach a goal. The goal is to position ourselves deeply in the will of God so that we can operate with the assistance of the Holy Spirit in our daily lives. The Holy Spirit enables us to face the daily challenges of life and respond in a Godly manner. But what does Sanctification mean?

The Sanctification Walk

It is amazing the level of agreement between various dictionaries on the meaning of the word *sanctify*. Merriam-Webster (being a trusted source) states that *sanctify* means: to set apart to a sacred use or to religious use, to free from sin, to impart sacredness, inviolability or respect to, or to make productive of holiness. Review of these meanings draws us to the following thought: The process of Sanctification centers on an act. In short, there is an action on our part that triggers the process and then that process must be completed. Is it by us or is it by someone else?

When you research the matter of sanctification as it relates to our relationship with God, we find the two occasions to discuss it have distinct names of reference. Dr. Norman G. Wilson in © The Wesleyan Advocate uses these two references. The first of them is instantaneous. The other is progressive.

The concept of instantaneous sanctification comes from the study of what occurs when we accept Christ as our personal Savior. We will explore salvation in later posts. For now we will disclose that in John 3:16 the Bible says, "For God so loved the world that he gave His only begotten Son. That whosoever believes on him should not perish, but have everlasting life." What is that all about? Well, in the 3rd chapter

Day 1 What Does Sanctification Mean to the Christian?

of Romans we find that there is no righteous or sin free person on earth. All of us have sinned and come short in God's eyes. In the 6th chapter of Romans we sadly find out that the penalty for sin is death, or eternal separation from God. Thankfully John 3:16 leaves us a promise for eternal life. Romans 10:9 tells us that if we believe in Jesus Christ, (basically in Who He is, what He did, that He lives, what He will do in the future and does daily on our behalf) then we will be saved. Take these two steps: believe in Christ and believe that God raised Him from the dead. Then the instantaneous sanctification happens. You were, (or if you haven't chosen Christ yet as your Savior can be) saved and have eternal Life. Through whom? Christ Jesus. That is instant. Right now; this should be good news for many people since we are a "right now" society.

    This brings us to the second reference, which is progressive. No it's not car insurance. But it is Life insurance, no doubt. Progressive sanctification occurs over the course of our lives and through a process. Colossians 2:6-10 unfolds a beautiful story of how Christians having received Christ should walk in Him. Following His example and taking His path. Then the Apostle Paul writes that we should be rooted and built up in Him. Wow, he has outlined for us that it is a process to become like Christ. It takes teaching, discipline and effort to become like Christ to move into our purpose of pleasing God, and to be sanctified for His use.

The point that the world wants to make on January 1st every year is, "Let's make a commitment to ourselves that we will stop doing or start doing something that makes us better." My point to Christians is let's start now seeking to live in God's will and by January 1st, we will be more disciplined. By living more like Christ, we will stop doing things that are not pleasing to God and start doing things that are. The end result is that we will be blessed beyond measure. Matthew 6:33 tells us to first seek the Kingdom of God and all its righteousness and everything else that we need will be given to us. Hebrews 13:21 indicates that God can and will make us "perfect in every good work." There is really nothing we can do except search God's Word for His plan, pray that His plan is made a reality in our lives and that we be given the grace to be who God wants us to be. Sanctification is not a "me" thing. It is a God thing. It's all about God and He can do so much in our lives if we learn to surrender to Him.

Day 1 What Does Sanctification Mean to the Christian?

I want you to be encouraged as we progress through the next three weeks. God is a merciful God Who chooses to take all of our sins and flaws and throw them into the sea of forgetfulness. If we ask for His forgiveness, the Bible says that He is faithful to forgive… (I John 1:9). The first step is to seek His forgiveness so that you and He can talk freely and He can move in your life without the barrier of sin in your way. After that, He will open your heart to much more than you ever imagined. Let's go forward in faith and trust in God.

OUR PRAYER:

God you are the Supreme Ruler and Creator of heaven and earth. There is none above You. As You created all of the universe, You created me. You created me for Your pleasure. You created me in Your image. Father, You created me fearfully and wonderfully in perfection. Sin has crept into our lives and Your children are far from You because of that sin. Forgive us, Lord. Forgive me, Lord. Remove everything that is not worthy of You. Whatever caused You to look away from me, Lord remove it. I want to have a righteous relationship with You. In these 21 days, strip me of everything that holds me back from a full relationship with You for You are my Father and my Healer. You are my Restorer. Restore me now and help me to sanctify myself to You. I want to belong to You and serve You more than I have ever served You before. In Jesus' Name, AMEN.

Day 2

A Solid Foundation

Yesterday we started off our "Sanctification Walk" just by understanding what *sanctification* means. We know that when we accepted Christ as our Lord and Savior we instantly received sanctification for our souls. We were freed from sin. Then we found out that there is a progressive sanctification. This is the process of growing in Christ and becoming what God would have us to be. God declares His Holiness and tells us to be holy because He is holy. We are to be separate and apart from the world.

In the 2nd chapter of Colossians, the Apostle Paul writes to the church at Colosse. A town that many would say was insignificant except that Paul took the time to write this letter to them. Paul focused on the deity of Christ and our duty to Him. In the 6th and 7th verse of chapter 2, Paul encourages us. He says, "6) As you have therefore received Christ Jesus the Lord, so walk ye in him. 7) Rooted and built up in him, and established in the faith, as ye have been taught, abounding therein with thanksgiving." If we are going to seek to establish a solid relationship with God, it must start in a place that would support it in the long term. If you know anything about agriculture or buildings, you know the first rule of both. In order for a plant to be sustainable, its roots must be able to reach deep into the soil and gather the nourishment necessary for the plant to grow. We know that any good building has a firm and strong foundation. Otherwise, we would have a pile of bricks and sticks because the building would fall.

Paul spoke to an issue that is very relevant to us today. The church at Colosse was in the midst of many perverse doctrines and cult movements. They were being challenged by the forces of evil that Christ had come to deliver us from. Today is not different. Merriam-Webster defines an idol as "a false god, a likeness of something; a pretender, imposter, a false conception." It is difficult to focus on the truth when there are so many false representations of the truth.

Day 2 A Solid Foundation

However, Jesus declared that He is the Way, the Truth and the Life. No man goes to the Father except through Him.

Man has been wandering around for generations looking for the piece to fill the void in their lives with something. Many of us recognize the popular ones: drugs, alcohol, sex, work and many other options that seem good. But the truth is that there are no good substitutes for what we really need. Follow me for minute as I try to draw a picture for you. We might have a taste for chocolate chip cookies. As a matter of fact it might be our most favorite food. If that is all we were to eat, our bodies would starve eventually, although it may take some time. We might feel good each day as we consume all the chocolate chip cookies we want, but eventually we would start gaining weight. Our bodies would begin to react to the lack of nutrition that would come from eating only chocolate cookies. Because we felt good for a time, we might even be inclined to rebuff anyone who tried to tell us that we were heading for health problems. "How can that be? I feel fine." Then one day, it all becomes clear to us as the effects of unhealthy eating and lack of nutrition manifest in our bodies.

The Sanctification Walk

This is how we are at some time or another. When we do not know Christ as we should we look for substitutes to take the place of Christ. Sadly, we do not realize that we are looking for a substitute for what we can have for free if we just ask. It seems like the Jehovah Witnesses have the answer. It seems like the Harikrishnas might as well. Perhaps you thought that the Buddhists have the answer. There is only one answer. That answer is in Christ Jesus. In the Bible God acknowledges our tendency to be easily swayed and drawn to things that are not of Him. Paul is led of the Spirit to warn the church at Colosse to be rooted and built up.

Consider the message that Paul was sharing. We know that Christ is the Answer. We know His ways are the example that God intends for us to follow. Keep it simple. If we are going to be sanctified, then we need to press toward the image of Christ. We need to allow God to mold our lives into what Christ set as the example: compassionate love for one another, the ability to lift up our brothers and sisters as they struggle through life; the ability to deny ourselves and strive for the fulfillment of God's will in our lives. If we study God's Word we establish the foundational advantage that we need to build our faith on. Think about the

Day 2 A Solid Foundation

sermons you have heard in your lifetime. Perhaps you have not heard a sermon but you have heard someone share God's Word.

The best way for you to establish your roots in faith is to study the Bible. Read it every day. Read the verse twice and then ask the Lord to show you how to apply it to your life. Believe it or not you can apply the Word to your daily life every day. A songwriter penned words that were immortalized by the great Mahalia Jackson. "Keep your Bible with you, read it every day, always count your blessings and always stop to pray. Learn to keep believing and faith will see you thro', seek to know contentment, and it will come to you."

Keep the faith and don't be discouraged. A personal note: I know that this is what God wants us to do. Satan has been trying to come against this "Sanctification Walk" like a mad man in desperation. The Bible tells us that Satan has no power except deception over us. If he can deceive us then he can convince us to do what he wants us to do. Otherwise, he can do nothing to us or affect our lives. Only you can give place to him. Just like the Christians in Colosse, we are faced constantly with options to move in directions that are not in God's will. We are being bombarded with false doctrine. Thus we are here now, seeking to move away from anything that is not of God. We want to separate ourselves from the worldly thinking that keeps us bound in sin. We want to put on Christ and be obedient to God in all of His Majesty.

OUR PRAYER:

Lord today we stand before You seeking Your forgiveness for all that we have done that is not in accordance with Your will. We repent of it , Lord. We have turned our backs on the things of this world. We recognize that we need to be rooted in the knowledge of Christ. He is the firm foundation upon which to build our lives. Christ is the last sacrifice that needed to be made for us. In that He died, was buried, raised by You and now sits at Your Right Hand, we are justified and sanctified in Your sight. Now let us live sanctified, set apart from the world and wholly committed to Your will.

    There are many that want to draw us away from You. Let us be able to see the lies that we are told. Reveal the enemy to us so that we can step back and allow You to fight him on our behalf. Let Your Word flow down into our very soul. Let us hide it there so that Your Spirit can call it into remembrance in the

Day 2 A Solid Foundation

hour we need it. Encourage us and hold us up with Your free Spirit. Protect us in the name of Your Precious Son, Jesus Christ. This is our prayer. AMEN.

Day 3

A Simple Prayer Will Do

Now that you know what it means to be sanctified and the reason we need to be set apart from the world's way of thinking, we can get into the meat and potatoes. Remember that we cannot sanctify ourselves without the Holy Spirit to help us. Our flesh is so weak that it cannot comprehend things in the spiritual realm. As Jesus put it in Matthew 26:41b, "The spirit is indeed willing, but the flesh is weak." We also know that sanctification is a part of the pathway to a deeper relationship with God.

John 15:7, "If ye abide in me and my words abide in you, ye shall ask what ye will and it shall be done unto you." What a promise from the Lord. Wow! Christ wants a relationship with you personally.

He counts you worthy to be in a relationship with Him. The Almighty, El Shaddai, Emmanuel, the Mighty Prince of Peace, Savior and deliverer wants to be in a relationship with you. Who are you? Simply put you are the "Whosoever" in John 3:16. The "all that have fallen short" in Romans 3:23; the lost sheep of the pasture that belongs to the Good Shepherd. That is who you are. That is who I am. That is who we are. Yet, Christ wants to get close to us and us to be close to Him; despite our short comings and flaws.

So how do we get close to Him? Through prayer. It was a little bit of a debate as to whether to discuss prayer first or to discuss bible study first. Prayer was the natural choice. Before you do anything in your life, you should pray. I Thessalonians 5:17 simply says, "Pray without ceasing." Matthew 26:41a is backed up by Luke 21:36, "Watch therefore, and pray always, that ye may be accounted worthy to escape all these things that shall come to pass, and to stand before the Son of man."

So according to God's instruction we should be praying all the time. We have a misconception about prayer. In our eyes we see great men of God standing before the congregation of worshippers praying great prayers of intercession on our behalf. They throw

Day 3 A Simple Prayer Will Do

strategic "Thou's" here and there. They use the word *Father* like a finely honed steel sword shining brilliantly as it is swung mightily at the once thought invincible enemy. The vision of these great men of God often intimidates us and makes us think to ourselves, "I can't pray like that. God surely would not hear me." Not so according to Matthew 6:5-6, "5And when you pray, you shall not be like the hypocrites: they love to pray standing in the synagogues and in the corners of the streets, so they are seen of men. Truly I say unto you, they have their reward. 6 But you, when you pray, enter into your closet, and when you have shut your door, pray to your Father, which is in secret; and your Father, which sees in secret, will reward you openly."

Prayer is not that difficult. All you are doing is talking to your Father. Plain talk that is sincere. God is looking for fervent and effectual prayer. That means you believe what you say and that God will answer you as you pray. You are not looking for God to answer in the manner that you want Him to respond. You are looking forward to God hearing and granting you what is best for you. Sometimes that means that we might not like God's answer. That is fine when we have faith that He will give us just what we need. So talk to Him like a friend that will watch your back. Talk to Him as a father who cares for and protects you. Talk to Him as the sovereign God He is that has a plan for you and will see it come to pass in your life. Talk to Him as if you know He loves you and you love Him. Most of all never stop praying. Before you put your feet on the floor every morning, you should thank God that you are able to breathe and have lived another day. The rest will easily come as you develop the habit of prayer which will turn into the lifestyle of prayer, which turns into prayer becoming a part of your character. Prayer should be so deeply engrained in you that people will look at you and know that you have a relationship with God.

Once you have uttered your first prayer of the day, do not stop. Just keep praying all day. When you pick out your clothes and have made the decision on what to wear. Look at it and say, "Thank you Lord for these clothes." That is a prayer. When you eat, never be ashamed to say grace over your food. If you eat with me, you can talk to me all you want until the food comes. Then you need to put it on pause. "Bless oh Lord these, thy gifts we are about to receive for the nourishment of our body, in Jesus' Name, Amen." Okay, you can continue talking to me now.

Day 3 A Simple Prayer Will Do

So today, concentrate on making your prayer life deliberate and on purpose. Say, "I am going to talk to the Lord today like an old friend." Keep in mind this simple reminder about how you should pray: A.C.T.S.

A - Acknowledge Who God is. Give Him the honor and the glory for being the Creator of the universe and the Maker of all things good. He is wise, He is powerful and He is above all else in the universe. God was, is and will be. He is the great I AM. Who is He to you? Well tell Him that is what He is to you. He loves to hear you talk lovingly to Him.

C - Confess your sins to Him. We already went over this, Saints. We all have sinned and come short of God's glory. There is none (Nobody) righteous. You get the point. If God already knows that we have sinned, what is keeping us from confessing it to Him? We can say we are sorry to many people. For some reason we have a hard time taking a moment and repenting to God. "Lord, I need You to forgive me. I don't want to sin against You." By confessing our sins we give God the chance to remove those sins. He wants us to come to Him and give our all to Him on the altar of sacrifice. A sacrifice is when we give up something to God for His glory and as an offering to Him. Pride is a very precious possession for all of us.

The Sanctification Walk

Pride means that we are holding onto a broken something and think that we can either go on without it being fixed or we can fix it ourselves. People are dying daily with a load of brokenness that they would not let God take away. Please don't do what we have done for so long. Don't put your sins on the altar and then pick them up when you leave. God is faithful to forgive us. However, we are terrible at repenting and forgiving ourselves.

T - Thank God for all that He has done for you. Psalm 100:4, "Enter his gates with thanksgiving, and into his courts with praise: be thankful unto him and bless his name." With our gratitude we get through the gates and praise keeps us in the court area or His Presence. Royalty traditionally sat on thrones. The palace consisted of outer walls that were meant to protect the king. Then there were several levels of security that you had to go through. Finally you got to the courts where the king was. In this Psalm we are taught that the way to enter into the Presence of the Lord is with thanksgiving. Come in saying thank You, Lord. Once you are in the gates it is appropriate to start praising the Lord. Now you are where God wants you to be. You are in His Presence, free to commune with Him, on a level that is above the troubles of the world.

Day 3 A Simple Prayer Will Do

He has you high above anything that will hold you down in the mess that you are praying about getting out of. This is not supposed to be a long lesson. But right about now I feel like dancing and giving God glory just for Him allowing me into His Presence.

Look how far we have come . We are speaking to the Most High God in humble adoration. We have confessed our sins to Him and He does the unthinkable, the Mighty God of Heaven reached down to our level and forgave us. In our thanksgiving we have slipped from a state of desire to be near Him until we have come, with invitation from the King, into the courts in a state of praise. Praise that moves us from our present circumstance into the presence of God. Hallelujah to God for opening up the way through Jesus Christ, our Lord. "I am the way, the truth and the Life. No man comes to the Father, but by me" (John 14:6).

S - Supplication. This is where we leave our requests on the altar for God to handle. Whatsoever you ask in My Name... Christ promised that if we ask anything in His Name it will be given to us. That is if we come to Him in the correct way. Prayer is a spiritual thing. That is the only place that prayer works from, our spiritual self. While we do not need to be able to pray like the great theologians and worship leaders of present day, we do need to be in a spiritual state of mind. Romans 8:5, "For they that are after the flesh do mind the things of the flesh; but they that are after the Spirit the things of the Spirit." At some point in this sanctification walk, you may feel the urging of the Spirit for you to release and let go so that God can truly move in your life. "Our weapons are not of this world but they are mighty through God." (2 Corinthians 10:4) Once we have made our requests known to God then all that is left is to trust that He will supply our every need. We are going to talk about the spirit later on.

OUR PRAYER:

God you are our great Creator and Provider of all things. Thank You for this day of prayer. Today we will pray humbly, deliberately and on purpose to Your glory. Help us to understand the ease in which we can talk to You. At the same time, help us to allow You to freely move in our lives. When we don't want to give up control it's a flesh thing. But we want to surrender to You more each day, Lord. So change our minds so we can give control to You, Lord, that's all we can ask for, the power of the Holy Spirit which gives us the

Day 3 A Simple Prayer Will Do

ability to speak to You all the day. Remind us at every opportunity to consult You on what we should say, where we should go and what we should do. We want to allow You to influence us at home, in the community, at school and on our jobs. We thank You for removing all the sin we have and deeply cleaning us, Your servants. Thank You, Father, for all that You have done and will do in our lives. AMEN.

Day 4

Finding Our Way Out of the Darkness

Imagine if you will, being in utter darkness. You have lost your way. You feel around for a reference in the touch of your hands. None of the darkness that you grab is familiar. There is no direction in the emptiness of your reach. As you struggle to find your way, you notice that there is no way. The path that you wish was there is a mystery to you. Its presence is not discernable in your limited state. There is no light. A voice pierces the night with words of comfort just when you think there is no hope. It calms your fears and draws you toward its source. As you move closer, darkness begins to recede. It yields to its nature and gives way to the light. The more you listen, the more a sense of peace builds up inside of you. You begin to have confidence in the voice. You start to trust its authority. In the realization that there is power in the voice, you halt. The very tone of it reveals the character of its owner. The light is brighter as time moves forward until, finally, you can see the path that was once unseen before you. Your steps are sure and your pace quickens. Your own movements are now reflecting the authority, power and comfort of the voice that lead you into its light. Warmth covers you and envelops your once isolated soul and it melts into oneness with the light. You then find yourself resting, no longer walking, at the feet of the voice and the light.

The Word of God is like the voice in our story. Sin separates us from God spiritually and physically. We do not realize that we know Him. We are not aware of the familiarity within our souls with His Voice and His Love. He placed a bit of Himself into us when He created us. The Bible says in Genesis that when He made man, He breathed into him the breath of life. From inside Him He breathed into man a soul. That is why we are so out of sorts when we are out of fellowship with God. That is how we are attracted to God

Day 4 Finding Our Way Out of the Darkness

and His direction. It is through the Word of God, the Holy Bible; we begin to know Him, His attributes and character. We begin to get a sense of what He would say about what we do. We learn His ways and His statutes. In short, we learn what Daddy will or will not accept.

2 Timothy 3:16 says, "All scripture is inspired by God and is good for doctrine, reproof, correction and instruction in righteousness." God said...ALL scripture. Therefore, you see in this short verse that we find the purpose of the Bible. Someone penned this little phrase. B-I-B-L-E, Basic Instruction Before Leaving Earth. When we enter into the right relationship with God, it is helpful to know how we can maintain that relationship. The understanding of the sanctification affirms our place in His plan and within His creation. Understanding the process of sanctification encourages us to keep going even when we don't want to. Understanding prayer opens the door to communicating with the Heavenly Father. Understanding the Bible opens our minds to the things of Heaven. Did you know that Heaven is our country of origin? That is where we began and where we will remain if we are truly sanctified through the precious gift of salvation. Then we

The Sanctification Walk

continue to grow through the daily process of sanctification to stay in fellowship with God.

Today's challenge is to pick up the Holy Bible, to start reading it, and to ask God to reveal to us how to search His Word for His instruction to us. 2 Timothy 2:15, "Study to show yourself approved unto God, a workman that doesn't need to be ashamed, rightly dividing the word of God." God does not want us to be ignorant. Ignorance is exactly where the Devil wants you. In Romans, we find the warning not to embrace ignorance because in ignorance there is a danger of trying to establish your own righteousness. Your own righteousness means that you do not have the righteousness of God. OUCH! That hurts. If the righteousness is anything but what God has prescribed, you are first in sin and then locked into idolatry. Have you considered that before? If you depend on your righteousness then that means that you are the god and your confidence and your worship is to yourself. Maybe it's not you but someone else that you are depending on. Whoever's righteousness you are hooked up in is where your heart and worship will be. This is very dangerous territory. It is also very dangerous territory for your testimony. We are warned to avoid false teachings. I

Day 4 Finding Our Way Out of the Darkness

am certain that we should avoid becoming false teachers as well as sitting under false teachers.

According to 2 Timothy 3:16, by studying the Bible, you will discover the truth about the Doctrine of God. A doctrine is simply a body of principles offered for belief. An example of a doctrine would be something like the Doctrine of no carbohydrates. Though not specifically based in religion, our example implies there is a belief being offered regarding the consumption of carbohydrates. So whatever logic or reasoning is offered in support of or against carbohydrates is intended to influence your life choice of whether to eat carbs or not. Paul admonished the ministers of God to ensure that they were preaching sound doctrine. Every preacher in the world should be overly sensitive of unsound doctrine. I am not suggesting fear of the actual doctrine. They should be afraid to allow the false doctrine to pass through their lips. Jesus said that it would be better for a man to have a millstone, (a real heavy rock) tied around his neck and cast into the sea than to lead one of his children astray. If you study the Bible, you will learn the principles of truth as God sees them. The Doctrine of salvation is how we obtain mercy and are regenerated by the gift of eternal Life. The Doctrine of spiritual gifts explains what God has to say about the giving, using and acceptance of His spiritual gifts. The Doctrine of love outlines how we are to love one another as Christ loved us. Doctrine is very important. It pretty much represents the standards and values of God. When the judgment happens, God will judge all creeds and opinions. The only thing that will stand is sound doctrine. Where do you find sound doctrine? In the Bible.

    Also, according to 2 Timothy 3:16, the scriptures are good for reproof. I would like to think of reproof as spiritual water repellant. Remember talking about God being Holy, so we must be Holy? This is our goal. Yes, we do have to contend with flesh as a constraint to our spiritual growth. That is why we have to be disciplined in the things of the Spirit. It is that type of discipline or quality control that drew me to sit down and share the Word of God with you through these writings. I have a million other things that I would otherwise be involved. However, as the Word is now in my heart through Bible study, I am committed and offer myself to do what God wants me to do. Through the Word, I am able to repel the foolish desires of my heart to watch the television reruns, over and over again. That would keep me away from this task that I am so honored to have in the Name of Jesus.

Day 4 Finding Our Way Out of the Darkness

As you read and earnestly study the Word of God a strange thing occurs. It begins to embed in our hearts and it does not go away. It remains there only for the Spirit to bring it back to our remembrance when we need it. Thus, when something comes up in our lives that would pull us toward our old ungodly ways, the Word calls us back into submission to God. David gave God such a sacrifice of personal commitment that he told God, "Thy word have I hidden in my heart, that I might not sin against thee." Psalms 119:11. The Word that is in you will repel the tricks of the enemy. I struggle with old ways, desires and tendencies every day. At first, it was very difficult to resist the devil. I would get discouraged and think that I was too far gone for God to have any part with me. Satan was so satisfied with this I imagined that he was laughing at me big time. If he had a Facebook account, it would have a picture of me and the comment, ROTF LMBO. The Word broke that bond and freed me to live in liberty for Christ and seek after things of the Spirit.

The Word of God is also good for correction. By definition, correction is the offering of something or substitution in the place of a mistake. There is a commercial in which giant gerbils sing "you can get with this, or you can get with that. You can get with this, or you can get with that." Daily that song plays out in our heads and hearts. We make choices for Christ and against Christ. Nevertheless, when the Word is in your heart it gives you suitable substitutes for some of the things that you are about to do that are wrong. Then it gives us a replacement for the mistakes we have made. The greatest example of a substitution for our mistakes is the death, burial and resurrection of our Lord and Savior Jesus Christ. What is beautiful about this transaction? The fact that in order to replace something or substitute something for something, something is removed. Through God's Word, this one truth is most important; our sins are removed by the gift of Jesus Christ. The blood covers, cleanses and blots out our sin. Better than Oxy-Clean, the blood removes the stain of sin. In place of sin, we have forgiveness, and restoration. There is a correction in the Word of God that heals and uplifts us.

Finally, Scriptures provide instruction in righteousness. If we are going to live Holy then we must know what living Holy looks like. We need a Guiding Voice in the darkness. We are familiar with the Ten Commandments. Living a Christian life is so much more than "Thou shalt not." There is more that you can do. We are encouraged to walk in our calling. We

Day 4 Finding Our Way Out of the Darkness

are strengthened by knowing that no weapon formed against us will prosper. We are identified as a royal priesthood. We are promised an eternal inheritance. We are afforded forgiveness for our sins. We hold a promissory note for a seat in the congregation of the righteous. It is through the Bible that we know that we can walk in accordance with our calling. The Bible is just like any other set of instructions that come with something you have to assemble. All of the instructions that I have seen have two components, what to DO to put your item together and the part we never read, the Cautionary Safety Message.

Be encouraged and read your Bible every day. Today's message is you can only progress in your Christian walk if you study the Bible. Never go without doing so. Just like prayer keeps you in touch with God, the Word does the same. Prayer is a conversation. The Bible is like a love letter. Do you like love letters? Well, the Bible is your personal love letter from God. As written in John 3:16, "For God so loved the world that he gave his only begotten son. That whosoever believeth in him should not perish, but have everlasting life."

The Sanctification Walk

OUR PRAYER:

Father, You are so awesome in all of Your ways. You provide for us beyond what our minds can imagine or comprehend. Today give me the ability to focus on Your Words to me that are in the Bible. Reveal to me through Your Holy Spirit the understanding that I need to apply Your Word to my heart and live a life pleasing to You. I thank You for Your doctrine, reproof, correction and instruction. With these things, I know that I can do all things through Christ Jesus.

As I learn of You, help me to reflect Your light and love to the world. Comfort me in Your correction. Empower me through Your doctrines. I don't want to be a Sunday morning Christian. I don't want to be just a seat warmer. I desire to be Your instrument of mercy in times of trouble. I desire to be Your angel in the time of need. I desire to be Your ambassador in time of ministry. I desire to be Your servant in the season of a calling.

I love You, Lord and adore You. Hear my prayer and keep me now. In the Name of Jesus I pray, AMEN.

Day 5

Get Out of Your Way!

When I was young I remember having a recurring dream where I would find myself in some kind of trouble and I needed to get away. In a myriad of scenarios, the theme was always the same. Someone or something was after me and I would try to run away. No matter how hard I tried, it seemed like I was running in place. The harder I ran the more I stayed in place. If I was in a hall, it was particularly evident that something was holding me back. The hall even appeared to stretch. As fast I would run the faster the hall stretched. In our quest to be what God wants us to be we often encounter the same challenge.

As we are trying to gain a deeper relationship with God by offering ourselves up to sanctification, there may come a point where we feel that we are not getting the traction we want. We are trying to move toward God, but it seems that the floor keeps moving under us. The hallway seems to extend before us. Our goal seems to be ever elusive. We don't seem to make any progress. Well, think about this for a minute. Is it possible that you are not really surrendering yourself to God?

We can't do anything by ourselves. The Bible says that we can do all things through Christ who strengthens us (Philippians 4:13). Jesus taught us in John 15:5 this golden gem of wisdom, "I am the vine and you are the branches. He that abides in me, and I in him, the same bears much fruit. For without me you can do nothing." Say that again, "Without me you can do nothing." Keeping in mind that our focus is our personal sanctification, this is a turning point. Up to this point we have shared how we need to be set apart for God's purposes. We talked about how we need to be rooted in the Word of God to stand against false doctrine. We then considered the power of prayer and then Bible Study. Perhaps now we are beginning to see the pattern of pursuit. I pray that you have come to the realization that we are nothing without the Father, Son and Holy Ghost.

Day 5 Get Out of Your Way!

Think about the last time you were in crisis. How about the time when you were in a fix and could not see your way out? You did not deserve mercy or the blessing that you got. The circumstances said there was going to be a certain outcome....But God. In the face of all of the things you have to go through the Bible declares promise after promise of deliverance, protection and restoration. How does that happen? How does it turn out good for the children of God? "And we know that all things work together for good to them that love God, to them who are called according to his purpose," Romans 8:28. God is capable of giving us "In spite of" blessings when everyone thinks we are counted out.

God wants to be everything in our lives. He wants to provide for us. He wants to protect us. He wants to heal us. He wants to be the Almighty God that He is in our lives without restraint. Just like the dreams, there is something holding us back. We want to run toward Him and there is no traction. We seek His face and we get close but never seem to see it. We want the Spirit to be around us and we just can't sit still long enough for it to come. God commits to the provision of all our needs. We commit to the status quo. Status Quo faith is counterproductive. It does not promote growth. It most assuredly does not foster a free flow of the spirit in our lives. Like hamsters running on a wheel we are satisfied to run forever and get nowhere fast. But true faith is evident in our action and it is through action that we are able to move forward in the blessings of God.

God wants to reign supreme in our lives so that He can work in our lives. He wants to make it better and then He receives the glory. So what is in our way? We are. Marianne Williamson wrote a wonderful poem of encouragement that I believe every Christian should learn by heart: Our Deepest Fear. She tells us that our deepest fear is not that we would fail. Our deepest fear is that we would succeed in life. That we would shine. She confronts the root of this fear by rightly stating that we are ashamed to be a success, to be blessed or to be anything positive because we think, "Who am I?" Well, you are a child of God. That is who you are. We belong to God in every sense of the word. He created us and we live in His universe and are subject to His divine power. If you want God to move in your life you need to learn how to yield to His will. Yield to His plan for your life and yield to the Spirit as He accomplishes His work. Stop going against the grain, and let God reign in your life.

Day 5 Get Out of Your Way!

Many people want God to heal them. Modern medicine is a marvel to say the least. The world looks at the developments of medicine and gives awards to doctors for their discoveries, etc. The doubting Christian looks at the circumstances and the hand of a surgeon. Once the circumstances are clear, they ask for healing but never accept the fact that God can heal. How do I know that? Glad you asked. Because after they pray about it, they talk to their friends and say things that reveal their mindset, "I went to the doctor and he says I have cancer." "It is hard living with this heart acting up; you just don't understand how hard it is for me with this condition." Do you hear the declaration of sickness in their words? If God says I'm healed, I'm healed. When we pray for healing we pray a prayer of faith. What does faith say except it is ready to embrace what is about to happen. Proverbs 18:21 says that Death and Life are in the power of the tongue. Romans has a little insight into the power of faith. I caution you though. Some people like to quote Romans 4:17 to say that if you just "Name it and Claim it" it will be. You have to read the rest of the 4th chapter. Abraham's faith is the issue and how at a time when the odds of any hope said not so, God said it is so. Thus, in the 17th verse it says, (in part) "...and calleth those things which be not as though they were." Then it goes on in the 18th verse to tell that "Abraham who against hope believed hope…" You see, in the case of Abraham, God had made a promise. And Abraham's attitude was the key to the promise being fulfilled.

Get out of your way. God wants to bless you in ways that you have never imagined or can ever comprehend. Your finances are a mess and you are trying to live for God. You are faithful in your service, your tithes and whatever else God has asked you to do. Yet you choose to still speak defeat into your life. You are in the way. Your doctor tells you that you have Diabetes and he tells you that you can reverse it and control it. You choose to feel bad for yourself and have a pity party, even though you asked God to heal you. You are in the way. You have been looking for a wife or husband. Your prayer has been "send me someone, Lord." When someone asks you about your pursuit of a mate, you say, "there is nobody out here for me." You are in the way. Whatever you have prayed for and seem to believe that God will do it for you, do not destroy the promise with your words. Don't glorify your circumstance with your words. Use your words to change your circumstances, instead.

Day 5 Get Out of Your Way!

What is the remedy for this spiritual ailment? Simply yield yourself to God and let Him work in your life. We cannot give place to our fears. We cannot speak against the prayers we are praying. We cannot allow our past to rule us. Flesh cannot see what the Spirit knows is about to happen. Satan does know that if he allows you to pray and to remain focused on God's Word he is sunk. He wants you off balance. He wants you to be distracted so the blessing will be delayed and you will be slowly destroyed by your circumstances. I could write for a month about being in the way of your own blessings from personal experience. As we are seeking to get closer to God, pride, fear, stubbornness and plain ignorance to the Word keep us locked in "worldly" thinking. God is calling you away from the world. He wants you to be separated from the world. He wants you to be set apart for His purposes. He wants you to be a heaven thinker. He is calling for you to be sanctified. But you have to yield to Him and let Him do the work in you that you long for Him to do.

Romans 12: 1, "Therefore, I urge you, brothers, in view of God's mercy, to offer your bodies as living sacrifices, holy and pleasing to God--this is your spiritual act of worship." What a beautiful offering to God, that we give our entire bodies, everything to Him. He would be so pleased to look upon the altar of our life and see us given by ourselves to Him to do what He will with us.

Elisha A. Hoffman penned the words to a very moving and popular hymn. "You have longed for sweet peace, and for faith to increase, and have earnestly, fervently prayed. But you cannot have rest or be perfectly blessed until all on the altar is laid." He goes on to write, "Is your all on the altar of sacrifice laid? Your heart does the spirit control? You can only be blessed and have peace and sweet rest, as you yield Him your body and soul."

Have you laid your all on the altar of sacrifice? God is calling you into your Holy state because He wants a deeper relationship with you. He wants it more than you do because He knows how wonderful it would be to have you back where you belong. He has seen what you can't even imagine. Is your all on the altar? Hoffman goes on to say, "O we never can know what the Lord will bestow of the blessings for which we have prayed. Till our body and soul He doth fully control and our all on the altar is laid."

Today, work on leaving your all on the altar. Every day we should put self on the cross and let it die

Day 5 Get Out of Your Way!

off. Truth be told there is no glory in your mortal bodies. The glory belongs to God and you will reap joy from giving yourself to God and letting Him create something new in you. Surrender everything within you today.

OUR PRAYER:

God, You have been good to us and have blessed us already in these five days. We honor You through our walk and talk. We reflect Your love and pray that You will keep the flames alive in our personal ministry.

Today we simply ask You to help us 'let go.' Help us to let go of our ego. The ego that makes us think we are able to take care of ourselves. Help us to let go of our fear. Lord we know that You love us and that You want to provide for us. Fear has gripped us and held us hostage far too long. Help us to let go of greed. You are the provider in this relationship. We don't need obscene extravagance. Help us to let go of this world's influence. Help us to let go of people that are holding us back from the relationship that we want in You. Help us Lord, Help us Lord, Help us Lord to be what You want us to be in spite of our circumstances. Just help us, because we cannot do it ourselves.

The Sanctification Walk

You are an awesome God able to do all things with anyone at any given time. We honor You and praise You for Who You are. Thank You for Your mercies and keeping power. AMEN.

Day 6

Let the Words of My Mouth

Picture this if you will. You are floating in the middle of a great ocean with no shore in sight. Your vessel is sure and solid. The provisions aboard are sufficient for your trip and your destination is reachable. The Captain of your vessel is capable and in firm command. There are no worries for you except to trust in your captain, stay put in your vessel and do what is necessary to keep the vessel moving, as the Captain requires. Your fare is paid and the way has been established for you. In the middle of your journey, you notice that there is a pistol in the boat. You examine it and start to think it is very interesting. The Captain warns you to be careful with it. It has a use and it should be kept for that purpose. You continue to flirt with a fascination with the power of the weapon. Despite several warnings to hold on to it for its intended use you dangerously flirt with the possibilities of its power. Finally, you can no longer keep it inside. You hold the weapon down and point it at the floor so as not to harm anyone and you pull the trigger. The weapon's loud report signals the damage of a loose round. A small hole appears in the boat and water starts to come in. You are thrilled with the discovery of what your newfound toy can do. Again, you pull the trigger not caring about the hole in the boat, comfortable with the safety that you have enjoyed, you pull the trigger repeatedly, much to the dismay of the Captain. He watches you make the choice to keep poking holes in your platform of safety. Finally, you realize that your ship is sinking. You look to the Captain, horrified. You say, "Captain the ship is sinking. Can you fix it and save me?"

How is it possible for us to be so caught up in our actions that we do not see the consequences right in front of us? From the outside looking in it seems so simple. Our passions come over us and we become blind to the effects of our actions. We miss the hidden effects that seem so obvious from without. We have often watched as friends and family head toward certain destruction and they fail to listen as we call to

Day 6 Let the Words of My Mouth

them to step back. Therefore, what makes us so different from them? Don't you see how we can be so consumed in our agendas that we are like the main character of our story? We engage in dangerous behaviors daily. Our actions are no fault of anyone other than ourselves. There is no place where this is more evident than with our mouths. Psalm 19:14 was one of the first verses that I memorized as a child. "Let the words of my mouth and the meditation of my heart, be acceptable in thy sight O Lord my strength and my redeemer."

The writer of the Psalm makes an assertion that is worth careful consideration. He brings to our attention the premise that our words and our heart are connected. He acknowledges for his own life the two are intertwined in an unbreakable relationship. At our most vulnerable times when we have all defenses down people see our inner most thoughts. We say exactly what is on our minds. That is where we get the saying 'think before you speak.' Someone suggested that we should guard our hearts. Then when we look in the Word of God we find that Solomon shares with his son this wisdom found in Proverbs 4:23, "Above all else, guard your heart for it is a wellspring of life." Guard your heart against what?

Our mouths are just like an exhaust pipe. Whatever is combusting in our hearts, within our soul comes out eventually as a product of our mouth. "Each one is tempted when, by his own evil desire, he is dragged away and enticed. Then, after desire has conceived, it gives birth to sin; and sin, when it is full-grown, gives birth to death" (James 1:14-15). Where does the conception of sin occur? In our hearts. Our hearts are connected to our mouths. We shared earlier that "the power of death and life is in the tongue," *or in the mouth.* (Proverbs 18:21)

It is amazing how much we either under estimate the power of the words that come out of our mouths or just plain disregard them. In our story, do you think that our passenger would have fired the gun once if they fully considered the effects of their actions? One could argue that if they had gone through the same experience before they would have been able to appreciate the scope of the situation. I submit to you that we constantly go through trials and tribulations. Most of which are the result of our own disobedience and sin. Yet, we still repeat the situation later on in life having forgotten about the results. Some of us are so bold to repeat behaviors willing to accept the outcomes as simply the cost of doing business. What

Day 6 Let the Words of My Mouth

in the world are you saying? Come on God. You are being hard on us with this Word right here. We have to face the facts. When we are called *sheep* in the Bible it is the most accurate representation of who we are that you can ever imagine. Sheep are dumb creatures that need the most supervision you could fathom. What kind of animal just wanders into the thickets and briars just because? Rabbits and others go in there to escape their predators. Sheep? What can you say about them? They wander away from the safety of the flock. They lose their way. Why do we disregard the danger associated with our words?

I hear you begging to hear some of the consequences of loose lips. Think about it, families destroyed. Words can destroy reputations of the innocent. Words can topple governments. Words can damage self-esteem. Words can cause doubt in the weak. Words can deceive people into believing things that are not true. Words can hit a person harder than any punch you throw. If you don't believe me Google "Teen kills self because of bullying." Try "Rumors of misconduct". Would you be surprised that there will be about 947,000 results in 0.19 seconds? Relationships can be killed in a fire of words both from within the relationship and outside of it. I think we have made the point that our words can result in a lot of damage. Sometimes what strangely looks like irreparable damage.

The point of this journey is to sanctify ourselves for the use of God's purpose. Keeping that in mind we have to look toward a hopeful theme for this discussion. God has given us a mouth for wonderful purposes. So in keeping our mouths from the evil that satan would have us to use it for, we must put it to work for the Lord. The first thing that we might consider is that the mouth is an effective witness to our love for God and His perfect plan for us.

The thoughts of man are hidden from other men until he reveals them to others. The Bible says that we, (Christians) will be known to the world by the love that we share for each other. The world will never come to God if they don't see the benefit and difference between the believers and the rest of the world. Our thoughts should be peaceful and loving toward others. We should be seeking the salvation of our friends and family. Our speech should be peculiar and indicate the high standard of the Kingdom. Do you know why the law is of no effect to a Christian? The answer: The law gives a standard to a sinner who has no other standard of conduct. For us, our standard is found in the Bible,

Day 6 Let the Words of My Mouth

which is above any earthly standard. That standard must be reflected in our words to those with whom we interact. Here is the encouragement that you should take away from this lesson. Use your words as an instrument of the Kingdom at all times. Psalm 34:1, "I will bless the Lord at all times, his praise shall continually be in my mouth." Every word that proceeds out of our mouths should glorify the Lord. They should always reflect the majesty, sovereignty and immutability of the Almighty God in heaven.

There is healing in our words. "Is there any sick among you, let him call on the elders so they can pray over him. Anointing him with oil in the name of the Lord." (James 5:14) Wonderful thing about healing is that it has many forms. Physical healing. Mental healing. Emotional healing. Relationship healing. Words spoken in the spirit have the ability to restore and lift up those who hear them. I can't tell you how many times I have spoken a Word at the direction of the Holy Spirit and without my knowledge I ministered to a specific need for the person that I shared it with. God can and will use you too in the same fashion. Wouldn't that be awesome?!

God wants to hear our worship in our words. In the face of adversity, we can speak peace into our lives.

This is especially true when we repeat the Scripture that we learned in Bible Study. "No weapon formed against me shall prosper." "We are more than conquerors through Jesus Christ our Lord." (Romans 8:37) "He is faithful to forgive." (1 John 1:9) "God so loved the world (ME) that he gave his only begotten son that whosoever (ME) believeth in him shall not perish but have everlasting life."(John 3:16) Donald Lawrence wrote a song that simply says, "Sometime you have to encourage yourself. Sometime you have to speak victory during the test. No matter how you feel, speak the word and you will be healed." Christians must stop accepting the labels of the world. Young ladies should never see themselves as worthy of the B-word label. Young men should never see themselves as thugs and gangstas. Television, radio, movies and pop culture do not define who a Christian is. In fact, they do not define who anyone is. When the Bible said that we are, "fearfully and wonderfully made," it is referring to all of creation. That is the definition of who you are. God made one man and out of the man formed one woman. He designed and created mankind for His purposes in decency and order. All of which was to glorify Him.

All of creation praises God daily in all that happens. Notice the trees when you come out of the

Day 6 Let the Words of My Mouth

house. They have their branches pointed toward heaven. Animals great and small yield to the work of the Lord and give way to His Presence. I recall once when I was standing in a small inlet on Maryland's upper Chesapeake Bay. I was unaware that there was a sudden change in atmospheric pressure. The change was so severe that it caused hurricane force winds on a beautiful sunny summer day. The birds in the air noticed though. It seemed that every bird in the area got up and flew away looking for cover. I thought it strange but gave it no more attention than a quick glance. Standing near me were some employees of the park where I was. The radio lit up with chatter warning of tremendous gusts of wind that knocked down trees and had caused havoc only a few miles east of us. They said the winds were headed our way. In fact within seconds the winds where I was went from a gentle breeze to 75 miles per hour in an instant. Did you notice how sensitive the birds were to the move of God? We should be so attentive. Just as there was a sudden shift in the atmosphere physically, God will shift the spirit realm suddenly to our benefit. In our attentiveness, we will be inspired to give up our praises to God. The love that we have for Him in our hearts will manifest and out of our mouths will come pleasing words. The praise that He so richly deserves and is waiting for and created us to give.

When we open our mouths it should be for committed holiness of speech. Every word that proceeds out of our mouths should give life. They should give honor to our God. James 3:2, (NLT) "We all make mistakes, but those who control their tongues can also control themselves in every other way." What an awesome promise and encouragement toward being Holy. Purpose to offer your mouth to God as an instrument of praise. Use it to glorify God always. Be sanctified in your mouth.

OUR PRAYER:

Dear God let the words of my mouth and the meditation of my heart be acceptable in thy sight O Lord, my strength and my redeemer. AMEN

Day 7

The Attitude Adjustment

L. Frank Baum wrote an endearing tale of a fictional girl from Kansas who dreamed dreams. In the course of the story, the girl encounters characters that we have all come to love. One in particular is the affable Scarecrow. He was a living personification of the old farmer's trick to scare off crows. A kindly man with a big heart, he was even courageous. His only down fall was that he thought he did not have a brain. Did you catch that one? He THOUGHT he did not have a Brain. Well how could he have thought if he had no brain? He even sang a song that I love to sing to myself even today. "I would not be just a nuffin', my head all full of stuffin' my heart all full of pain. I would dance and be merry; life would be a ding-a-derry, if I only had a brain." Life would be a ding-a-derry. Life would be great if we used the brain that we have.

Eventually the Scarecrow found out he did have a brain. He was so consumed with the thought that he did not have a brain, he never stopped to think, "I couldn't have a thought if I didn't have a brain." Once he realized he had a brain, he started living as though he had a brain. His attitude changed. It was positive and upbeat and he had confidence in himself and his ability to think thoughts. He did not become another Lincoln; he was the best Scarecrow that Scarecrow could be. Our thoughts get so jumbled up sometimes that we allow the enemy to come in and plant what a dear friend of mine, Doris Lyles, calls thought bombs. BOOM! The next thing you know your thoughts are out of sync with who you really are. We talked about who you really are at the beginning of the week. My daughter, Samia, calls it the "Battle between Your Ears." That battle shapes our attitude. Today it is our attitude that we must sanctify.

Philippians 2:5, "Let this mind be in you that was also in Christ Jesus." (KJV) In the New Living Translation, it is made plain, "Your attitude should be the same that Christ Jesus had." Paul spent his time in writing to the church at Philippi promoting unity in the

Day 7 The Attitude Adjustment

spirit and in the church. Paul's point, the Kingdom of God is unified in thought and attitude toward the things of the Spirit. That makes sense, doesn't it? If we are about the Kingdom of God and living in the power of the Holy Spirit, then we should be focused and on a spiritual plane. This is what I call Heaven thinking.

In God, there is no confusion. I Corinthians 14:33, "For God is not the author of confusion, but of peace, as in all churches of the saints." In Psalm 133:1, the psalmist writes, "Behold, how good and how pleasant it is for brethren to dwell together in unity!" God wants all of His children to be in harmony with each other. That harmony is oneness of mind. It is oneness of attitude and oneness of purpose. Sanctify our attitudes and you have half the battle won. Consider the principles of electricity. For electricity to flow through wires and appliances some things must exist: conductivity, continuity and capacity.

Conductivity in our attitudes fosters sharing of the Holy Spirit. The Spirit needs to flow. Romans 14:19, "So then, we must aim at those things which bring peace and that help strengthen one another." Our attitudes should bring peace to the body of Christ and strength to our fellow Christians. That is conductivity. Our attitudes have the power to, as old preachers would say, carry the love of Christ from heart to heart and breast to breast. Have you ever been in a worship service but not really "in the mood?" You went because there was an urging in your spirit to go. That was God drawing you. As the service progresses, the songs go forth, prayers are uttered and testimonies are shared. As the atmosphere becomes charged, you begin to feel the move of the Spirit stirring in your spirit. You don't know why, but you leave feeling rejuvenated in your heart. You feel better. What happened? The oneness of the body allowed the reassurance of the Lord's grace and mercy to flow through the place of worship. As you stood there it was as if you had been standing between two huge wires, one positive and the other negative. Somewhere in your heart the circuit was completed and you became a part of the flow in the Spirit. On those special occasions when everyone is on one accord, the Presence of the Lord visits our worship.

Continuity is where like-mindedness meets the loneliness we sometimes feel. It is where the enemy is defeated when he tries to pull us away from the Lord. AC and DC current are very different. AC appliances do not run on DC. AC means alternating current or the electricity flows in two directions. DC flows only in

Day 7 The Attitude Adjustment

one direction. Our homes are powered by AC. Portable radios are powered with DC. AC is much stronger. Stay with me on this one. DC eventually runs down and needs to be recharged. At some point the DC Battery has no power and the appliance has no power. They both are there dead without any life. But AC flows from power sources that seem perpetual and unending. It flows back and forth. DC reminds me of Satan. He sucks us dry of the power that God has given us. The only way that Satan has power over us is when we give it to him. He uses us like little batteries for his folly. Just so he can watch us be drained of our power. When we have no power he has no use for us and he seeks out some other batteries to drain. But when we are connected to Jesus, He is the giver of life. He can give it to us more abundantly and everlasting. The only way that we are cut off from Him is when we are out of sync. Our attitude is not consistent with His will and thus we are out of continuity. I can recall several times while at work we lost partial power. Some equipment worked while others did not. When the electrician arrived he told us that we had lost one phase of power. We were not running on full power. It was not until we gained back the other half of the power that everything worked as it should. God never loses

The Sanctification Walk

His power. It just doesn't happen. But when we humble ourselves before the Lord and seek Him, now we are completing both phases of power, heaven and heart.

Capacity is the amount of electricity that we can hold. All wiring, electrical components and appliances have a maximum capacity for power. If you do not have enough power, then the appliance will not run. There is just too little to run the appliance. Every appliance draws a certain amount of electricity. If that amount is not present it does not work. Sometimes our attitudes leave the body of Christ short on our personal contribution. It is almost as if we are non-existent. If someone put a meter on us, could they detect that we were there? Likewise, every appliance has a maximum capacity of electricity that it can hold. Electrical appliances have components that take the full force of the AC that comes into it and then it "Handles" the electricity allowing only that which is necessary to run the appliance and it stores the overage in a way that protects the appliance. If we are closed minded in our attitude we will never receive the full power that God has for us. We also need protection from the full power of God. We are not in our perfected bodies just yet. Moses insisted that God show Himself so that

Day 7 The Attitude Adjustment

Moses could see Him. God told Moses that he was not ready for that kind of wide-open glory. No Moses, you aren't prepared to receive My full power yet. Flesh just can't handle all of God at one time. Because we are still in our mortal bodies God's full Presence would blow us up like an unprotected appliance plugged up directly to the transformers outside of our houses. When we have the proper attitude for Christ, we hold flesh in restraint and allow the fullness of our spirit man to come forth. That is when we are at a point to handle more of the Presence of God. Isn't that awesome? The prospect of being in the Presence of God and enjoying Him.

I wonder what it would have been like if Christ had a different attitude? This would probably have been the result. Mercy would be an unknown term. The Bible tells us that "The wages of Sin is death" (It would stop there, finished). But, with Christ's attitude it goes on to state, "But the gift of God is everlasting life through Jesus Christ our Lord." (Romans 6:23)

If Christ had a different attitude, Judgment would be swift and all of us would be judged. Hebrews 9:27, "it is appointed unto man once to die and after that the judgment." Right there we would be dead. Notice the trend in the first half of Romans 6:23 and then this, we are counted as sheep for the slaughter. However, God's mercy continues beyond condemnation and takes us to redemption. Now let's look at Hebrews 9:28, "So Christ was once offered to bear the sins of many; and unto them that look for him shall he appear the second time without sin unto salvation." So it is that acceptance of Christ's gift which results in our salvation. We are saved from the judgment.

If Christ had a different attitude God's emotion would rule over his reason. God desires that we be redeemed and not destroyed. But if He was offended by our disregard for His rules instead of being merciful we would surely be lost. Could you imagine if God did not put His anger to rest? We are talking about the God who simply spoke and life began. A universe was formed. When you get angry doesn't your voice raise in volume. Is it nurturing and peaceful; or, is your voice loud and stern? I would not want to be on the receiving end of God's anger. Once He said let there be light and the entire universe lit up. Just a Word from the Creator has such power, I would not want to hear the Word of His wrath.

Compassion would not exist. The cross would have been of no effect. Christ is the only person that made it what it was, the table upon which our salvation

Day 7 The Attitude Adjustment

was crafted and sealed. Christ's blood would never have touched air. Not a drop would have been shed for you and for me. I would be lost. All because Christ's attitude would not have been mercifully turned toward me. As deeply stained with sin as I was, cleansing would not have been an option. My hope for a future would be a futile search for a cool place in the lake of fire where I would be consumed with all of those who were not redeemed.

Given the cost that was paid for me to allow me to have a right attitude, I can sanctify my attitude. Lord, You can have my mind and my body and soul. I can yield my will long enough to allow You to work in me. I can do nothing without You. It will take Your awesome power. My attitude knows Who You are and what You can do. In 1886, Carl Bobert penned one of the greatest hymns of our time. His attitude is captured in its words:

"O Lord my God, when I in awesome wonder, consider all the worlds thy hands have made; I see the stars, I hear the rolling thunder, thy power throughout the universe displayed. Then sings my soul, my Savior God, to thee; How great thou art, How great thou art. Then sings my soul, my Savior God, to thee; How great thou art, how great thou art!" Those words were written by Carl Gustav Boberg circa 1885.

In Nehemiah 8:6, "Ezra praised the LORD, the great God; and all the people lifted their hands and responded, 'Amen! Amen!' Then they bowed down and worshiped the LORD with their faces to the ground." Based on that powerful scripture, the great late Andre Crouch wrote a song that should be the anthem of the unified Church under Jesus Christ. It simply says **"Let the Church say Amen, Let the Church say Amen. God has spoken, let the Church say Amen. Make this your response to whatever he says; From the healing of your body to the raising of the dead; No matter how you feel or how your world is reeling; Battle on through the night, cause you're gonna win the fight; Even in the valley, or standing at your Red Sea; Continue to say Amen cause your help is on the way. God has spoken, let the Church say Amen.**

OUR PRAYER:

God of heaven hear our prayer today. You alone are able to grant us this humble request. There is none above You, nor is one worthy of the glory that is due to

Day 7 The Attitude Adjustment

You. We need You to break down flesh in the Name of Jesus Christ. Remove prideful attitudes. Displace our egos. Destroy the confidence in the world that keeps our attitudes from You. Anoint with Your Holy Spirit our eyes that we may see and know the tricks of the enemy. Sharpen our ears that we can hear and distinguish Your Voice. We need You to do this for us. We can't do it by ourselves.

Making it personal Lord, Sanctify my attitude unto You. Sanctify it to where no matter what is going on in my life I can offer praise. Sanctify my attitude unto You so that even in the face of my enemies I can offer my worship. Sanctify my attitude unto You so that my first thought is of You and Your glorious Kingdom. Sanctify my thoughts so that I can see You working in me, around me and for me. I want my attitude to be in synchronization with Your will and Holy Spirit. Amen.

Day 8

Give it ALL You've Got

I Thessalonians 5:23, says, "And the very God of peace sanctify you wholly; and I pray God your whole spirit and soul and body be preserved blameless unto the coming of our Lord Jesus Christ." "Sanctify you wholly," "Preserved." What is God trying to tell us in this portion of Scripture?

In the fifth chapter of First Thessalonians Paul is attempting to encourage the readers of the letter to always be prepared for the coming of Christ. Since nobody knows the day or the hour that Christ is coming back, it is to our best advantage to be prepared for His arrival always. Paul's concern was that all of the brothers (and sisters), (those who have accepted Christ) make sure they are in position for a quick exit from earth at the hand of our Savior. Good advice for the Church in times when it seems that we are so easily distracted from the Cross and saddled with sin.

Let's face it; Christians are tempted like everyone else. In our current pop culture, we have a tendency to lose focus on everything. We have distracted driving, inattentive conversations, failure to observe our surroundings and failure to pay attention to our kids as they live their lives. We just plain don't pay attention to the important stuff in life. We can describe it as a sort of Spiritual hyperactivity or as we commonly know it, ADHD. Paul says we have to change that. We must be disciplined in the Spirit. He prayed that God would sanctify us, as the New International Version of this scripture says, through and through. Part of the sanctification process is to WATCH and pray. In Matthew 26:36-46 we find Christ and the disciples, minus Judas, in the Garden of Gethsemane. Christ in this moment finds a lesson to share with the disciples who are falling asleep while the enemy is on the way. In verse 41 Christ says, "Watch and pray so that you will not fall into temptation. The Spirit is willing but the body is weak." Isn't that pretty much us every day?

We must be vigilant in our daily lives to guard against temptation. Keep your eyes open for tricks of

Day 8 Give it ALL You've Got

the enemy. Remember it is not the temptation that condemns us; it is the yielding to temptation that causes us to sin. If I can take you to Genesis for a moment we will see how that happens. In the third chapter, we see the quick fall of man into sin. Satan tempted the woman. She was convinced that it was good and ate it. So she gave it to her husband. He listened to his wife over God. When the two of them both had eaten the fruit that is when the sin manifested. The two of them agreed. I want to introduce a thought to you for your careful and prayerful consideration. As the man and woman agreed which sent all flesh into a sin state, think for a moment when temptation enters your heart. When you act on it, your flesh is pushing your spirit to commit the sin. Follow me on this line of thinking for just a moment. As we commit sin, it becomes a conspiracy between our flesh and our spirit. The flesh is conspiring against the spirit and if in the spirit we yield to or agree to the plan of the flesh we are damaged in our spirit. That is where sanctification comes into play. If we are sanctified in our spirit, our spirit man will be strong enough to bring the flesh into subjection. There we are able to obey the direction of the Word of God to resist the devil so that he will flee, "Preserved blameless unto the coming of our Lord Jesus Christ."

In short, Paul was encouraging us to allow God to lead us through our lives and be a part of every aspect of our lives that sin would not enter into it. If we allow God to reign in our lives then sin will not have room to dwell. This is the very essence of setting ourselves apart for God's will and pleasure. We will begin to live in the growth of the Holy Spirit. Our divine nature will be revealed and we will then begin to operate in the holiness of the righteousness of God. We won't be without sin, but we will strive to be sinless. We will continuously seek forgiveness and consciously avoid anything that is not of God. We will be right where God wants and expects us to be: in the process of sanctification, striving to be Holy and acceptable in the eyes of the Lord, daily.

When we started this journey we consciously offered ourselves as a living sacrifice unto God. At this point, you should not only be reading these lessons, you should also be reading your Bible daily seeking His guidance for living our lives. You should also be in daily prayer seeking His Presence and a relationship with Him. This week we will talk in depth about worship, giving Him the praise that is due to Him and

Day 8 Give it ALL You've Got

honoring Him in all of our activities and decisions. Remember the thought behind this great effort is to yield to the power of God and allow Him to sanctify us through and through.

A thought comes to mind as we are sharing in this great experience. If you are looking for a change in your life for the benefit of your eternal soul, then you must commit to it with your whole heart. When Christ died on the cross for you, He didn't "kind of" or "sort of" die for you. He died for you. He declared on the cross, "It is finished." The work was completed on Calvary's cross to pay our sin debt. Then He was buried in the grave for three days and rose in fulfillment of the prophecies of His death, burial, and resurrection.

I am reminded of this story. A Pig and Chicken were walking through town one sunny Saturday morning. They passed a church with a sign out front. It said, "Bacon and Egg Fellowship Breakfast." The Chicken said, "Oh boy! Let's go make a donation toward the breakfast." The Pig replied, "For you it is a donation. For me it is a life commitment." How far are you willing to go with the Sanctification Walk? We have been walking for a week now. Don't give up if you find it hard to stay the course. Too many times we have been on the brink of a breakthrough and given up. That is the usual approach. There is a saying that goes like this, "If you want change but do the same thing as you have always done and expect an outcome different than it has always been, that is insanity." If you want a change in your life you are going to have to do something that you have never done before. To get farther, you have to go farther. I find that it is just past what you think you are able to do that you find out how much more you can do.

Don't turn back now. Don't give in to temptation. If you are fading and it is hard to keep going on this journey, drop to your knees. Go to God in prayer and don't get up until you reach out to God and feel His strength moving over you. He can do it. He will do it if you ask. Sanctification is a great achievement. It makes sense that it will take resolve on your part to obtain it.

OUR PRAYER:

Merciful Father in heaven; You Lord Who alone has all power in heaven and earth we come to You humbly and without our own power. Father we submit to You

Day 8 Give it ALL You've Got

and ask that You forgive us of every sin that we have committed.

We have been seeking sanctification of our selves this week. We want to be separated from the world system in our lives. We want to be Heaven thinkers and not World thinkers. We crucify self and turn from our own selfish desires. Give us the strength to continue in Your Name. Help us to remain focused on stretching beyond our view of our limits. We know that we can do ALL things through Christ Who strengthens us. Making it personal Lord, I am more than a conqueror. Now I declare that I am a conqueror over my flesh and want Your Spirit to reign in my life. Take me now Lord and cover me with Your love. In Jesus' Name I pray, AMEN.

Day 9

Now Faith Is

Special Note: I prayed over the faith lesson for several days. This chapter is so important that God gives us the following direction in Hebrews 11:6, "But without faith it is impossible to please him: for he that cometh to God must believe that he is, and that he is a rewarder of them that diligently seek him." I must confess that I have resisted using something that I wrote a long time ago. It is a tribute to my mother. Children are not given the opportunity to choose their parents. I thank God every day that I am alive for the blessing to have this woman as my mother. Some children measure their mother's love and affection based upon availability. Some children measure the worth of their mother by the worth of the things given. I cherish my mother based upon the spiritual example that she gave me. The greatest lesson that she gave me was faith. In my life, I have had tremendous pain and the only thing that I could do was depend on God. It was faith that brought me through. If my mother could believe in God and trust Him, I think we all can believe and trust in Him. Please meditate on this story for a moment.

Hebrews 11:1 in the Holy Bible, (King James Version) says; "now faith is the substance of things hoped for, the evidence of things not seen." When we first shared the original version of the Sanctification Walk we saw many posts about family members battling cancer for years. Today, I learned about a dear friend diagnosed with cancer. He now joins the ranks of so many people that have faced such a trial in their lives. There is not much to say when a person is facing dire health issues, daily. I know this from the perspective of an intimate spectator while my mother suffered under the pain of Sickle Cell Anemia and Muscular Sclerosis. In 2014 my mother-in-law succumbed to Metastatic Breast Cancer. She fought for eight years, and fought well I might add. I have had to face such terrible circumstances for more than three quarters of my life.

Day 9 Now Faith Is

But, I guess you could say that I have not experienced anything for myself. That is not true. If you are an immediate family member, the pain is yours, too. The only thing I missed was the treatments. Still I had a front row seat. I must acknowledge that God perhaps has allowed me to go through these experiences to help another person who is watching a loved one face death down with the sole purpose of winning. Perhaps what my mother and my mother-in-law taught me will help someone who is going through their trial. I offer this one thought: in the midst of the storm, as long as you have breath in your body, you can have faith. No matter what your circumstances are, you can have faith.

Faith has a proven track record. Some would submit to me that faith is an abstract, surreal concept that only speaks to attitude and nothing of substance. I tell you not so. I could tell you what the word faith has meant in my life. In 1944, my mother was diagnosed with Sickle Cell at the age of two. Her parents were told that she would be dead by age 21. There would be no hope of having children or major surgeries after the age of 17. In short her life would be a sheltered one littered with many doctor visits, most of which were in relation to experiments to find out about this enigmatic condition at the time. Sports and normal activities of a child would be out of the question. Just getting through the trials of academia would be a monumental achievement. The pain would be unbearable and crippling by itself, let alone the physical changes her body would go through. That is what the doctors said.

My mom did spend a lot of time in doctors' offices. She was studied, examined and reported on. She spent my early years in and out of the then Freedman's Hospital, (now Howard University Hospital). One day, they told me that she had to go to a State hospital in Hagerstown, Maryland. The inference was that she was going there to get good care, be kept comfortable, and then die. I was six at the time. Nobody thought that I could understand this concept. Wrong! I did. They were sending my mom to a hospital far away so she could die there. Or so they thought.

Please do not get me wrong, my family did not give up hope on my mother. They just could not see any other outcome. Oddly, my mom saw a very different one. It is not spoken of much, but my mother lived in some pretty desolate conditions. She lived for 20 years in a hospital full of tracheotomy patients, (people with breathing tubes in their throats) paraplegics and bed-ridden souls. It smelled of death and declining health all around. It was not pleasant. She told me she

Day 9 Now Faith Is

was terrified as some patients were not well cared for. She even suspected that neglect had contributed to some of their deaths. She was on a ward where there were 5 other patients. The décor, if you can call it that, was drab. It looked awful. She even considered suicide on several occasions rather than live through all of this. Despite its looks, for my mother, it was not a ditch in which to die. Much like Joseph, her ditch was a platform for many miracles to happen.

One day I will write a book about her life and contributions to the people around her and the community. I am sure that many may never have known her. But, for the purpose of this book, I will offer just this brief glimpse into her world.

My mother somehow found the strength in God to live for Him in even in the midst of her private hell. She discovered that the diagnosis did not define her. The limitations of medical treatment did not mold her destiny. The inability to afford in-home care and a private nurse did not diminish her importance to a greater calling. She realized that in Christ she had a purpose and a duty. I often teach that worship is a misunderstood term. It is thought somehow to just encompass a church building for congregational activities. We worship God when we acknowledge Who He is in our lives. Everything we do in a day has the potential to be worship. Perhaps she knew this and perhaps she did not. Barbara Offer's life became worship to God. Since there seemed to be not much else to do but wallow in self-pity and act defeated, she decided to find something constructive to do. This is where the miracles begin.

She looked back on her life and found that not only had she had a fulfilling school life and participated in plenty of activities, she had many other accomplishments. She owned her own business, was a model, she did have several successful surgeries past age 17 and at the age of 22 she gave birth to me. The next time you see me, stop and take a good look. Look at me and see that I have all of my fingers and toes. I am intelligent and articulate. I have been blessed to attain success in my profession as well as in the ministry. I have been anointed as a vessel of God to minister to people that sometimes I will never see face to face. I have ministered on radio, television, the internet, in person and in numerous other ways. All of this is the result of a seed that sprang forth out of Barbara Offer: a chosen vessel for the time that she was with us. Looking back and seeing how God had blessed her, she was His special tool to reach others who were going through similar

Day 9 Now Faith Is

situations. Her assignment was to minister. Through the pain, discouraging moments, and through all the skepticism, she found her faith and her joy. Knowing that God chose her brought encouragement. Ultimately, she became an encourager.

She got so comfortable with the prospect that God was really using her that she took on a project that the State of Maryland could not do. While at the Western Maryland Medical Center in Hagerstown, she decided that it was unacceptable to have no decorations in the hospital. Drab lifeless walls were not fitting of her and her fellow patients. They formed a patient's advisory group to air concerns to the administration of the hospital. They petitioned to change the decor and atmosphere. Then Maryland said, "We don't have the money." She asked, "Can we raise the money?" With the permission of the State, a foundation was established and fundraising began. Within a few short years the hospital was transformed into a beautiful place where people could be cared for with dignity and grace. Her campaign carried her to venues outside of the hospital to tell the community about what they were doing and to solicit involvement. The response was grand. Businesses, non-profits, community organizations and citizens from all over the State and region

The Sanctification Walk

contributed and made it all possible. You may say that was a great accomplishment. But, she had one more dream. Through faith miracles still happen.

Barbara Offer was determined that she was going to see her first grandchild and walk. She spoke it and declared it with authority. Then she set out to achieve it. She told her doctors that she wanted to get on track to walk again. They did a procedure to straighten out her folded legs, and they put her in physical therapy. Although she had not walked in over 15 years, she was on her way. In her lifetime, she had been blind, deaf and even quadriplegic. She began to stare down her condition and declared that despite what anyone thought, she was going to walk. She prayed day in and day out. She taught the Word of God to those who needed to hear it. She always gave testimony of how God was blessing her. He was blessing her from the wheelchair, and the bed. This is faith in action.

At the same time, I had married and everyone was waiting on the arrival of my first child. Monique and I took our time. As it would happen, mom took her first steps out of the wheelchair right about the time Monique would get pregnant. Later that same year, my 47-year-old mother packed all her stuff and

Day 9 Now Faith Is

left the Western Maryland Medical Center to come home. Remember she was supposed to die 26 years earlier. It was a super homecoming for her. It was as if a celebrity had come to town. Many people visited the house for months on end. Finally, she was able to give her testimony of how God had brought her through so much trial and tribulation with her condition. We had classified her condition wrongly. Because we had classified it wrong our expectations were wrong. Her condition was not a health condition. It was a spiritual condition. Just like Joseph was thrown into a pit and he rose to a life of spiritual and physical prosperity. My mother was thrown into a pit with not one but two debilitating and terminal diseases. She had to learn to trust God. There was no one else to trust. Then she began to work for God. She continued to work for God for two more years beyond when she left Hagerstown. Finally, at age 49 it was her time to leave us and go home to the Lord. This we all must do, one day. But first, my mother did what God wanted her to do, and then He fulfilled the promises He made to her.

As we shared earlier, in Proverbs it says, "Death and Life are in the power of the tongue…" We speak what we believe and what we speak has awesome power. We must speak encouragement over ourselves in the confidence of the Lord Jesus Christ. My mother found that faith was not only a belief, it was action and purpose unwavering. She believed without a doubt that the joy of the Lord was her strength. She found that it did not matter how she was treated in the hospital, God would always treat her well. Barbara Offer found out that it did not matter what the doctors said. It was more important what God says. Even though her family feared that she would die, she overcame the fear that she would die. She believed in a promise and then she learned to live in the promise. That is faith. She demonstrated the substance of things hoped for. She accepted and took personal notice that each day she had an opportunity to reach her goal was evidence of things not seen. God is good. He is the same God that has control over the lives of anyone else who may be suffering with cancer, MS or whatever ailment there may be!

OUR PRAYER:

Merciful and wise Father, Creator of all that is good, we thank You for Your divine plans in our lives. You have ordained a destiny for us if we just yield ourselves to Your will. The tool that You have given us to remain

Day 9 Now Faith Is

in You and allow You to work a work in our lives is faith.

Strengthen and cultivate the faith in me Lord that I might overcome flesh and see in the Spirit what You are able to do, going to do and have promised to do in my life. Lord, a life yielded to You is a life that is sanctified and holy before You. Allow me to embrace the character of a faithful servant.

May my actions and confidence in You translate into a testimony that others might see You in me and Your great works. Not that I be glorified, but that You would be glorified in my life before the world, AMEN.

Day 10

Peace like a River

All I want to do is get some rest, but there never seems to be enough time. I would go to work and the boss constantly had things for me to do. There were things in the morning and in the afternoon. He had things waiting when I finished what he had already given to me. And sometimes he had things that he wanted done NOW and then he gave me things that he wanted done now MORE than the other things that were urgent. And don't get me started on home. Every two weeks I got a paycheck. At one time my spouse lost her job and we were working on one income. Therefore, we had to work really hard to keep up. Sometimes things had to wait until the timing is right to be paid. When I got home from work after being with my insensitive boss, there was always a crisis that I needed to solve…right then. Don't get me wrong, I love my family. I put up with my boss. Because I love them, I listen to every problem. Some problems are for me to solve. Others are just for me to listen to. At least that's what marriage counselors tell me I should watch out for when my spouse "vents." Which reminds me, 'why do I spend most of my time trying to figure out what I am supposed to do?' It usually takes more time for me to figure that out than it does to do the tasks. Problem is that when I figure out what I am supposed to do, I run out of time to do what I am supposed to do. This means that now I have to rush to get it done! However, I must pay close attention so that I do it right. Anything done wrong will have to be done again. Go figure. Oops, that takes time. Once I have all the issues resolved, (At least the ones I am supposed to have solved) for my boss, my spouse and my kids, I began to start thinking about solving the issues that are important to me personally. Darn, is that the timer going off telling me that I don't have enough time in the day?!

Is that the way your day seems to you? Time management is an elusive animal. Then you have that one person in your life that has no family, apparently no life and they say something profound to you like,

Day 10 Peace Like a River

'you've got too much going on in your life.' Duh! So what should I eliminate? My spouse? Maybe I can put my kids on eBay. I could start telling my boss that he is an idiot for assigning me too much work at one time. I could use those bills to wallpaper my bathroom. Have you ever gotten to that point in your life where you just wish it would all stop just for a minute? A week of vacation is just enough to get you away from the job to focus on the issues at home. Even if you and family go away, it takes you three days to get unwound from work and then you spend the last two days thinking about returning to work and the hectic schedules maintained at home.

    This is probably the most relevant issue facing Christians today. How do I have peace in the midst of all the confusion of everyday life? How can Christ actually get rid of all of this confusion? There is a promise in the Word of God, found in Isaiah 26:3, "You will keep in perfect peace him whose mind is steadfast, because he trusts in you." Isaiah declared to God his confidence in a promise for peace.

    How then should we achieve this peace? Before we get to that, we must rewind a little bit. We just discussed getting out of our own way. In our scenario, we truly have the power to overcome the circumstances that we are facing. Our power lies in the confidence that we see displayed by Isaiah. We must know in our hearts that God is able to do all things. Why don't we know this? We have a hard time wrapping our heads around God's infinite power in large because we doubt. Doubt is the evidence of spiritual weakness. We talked about faith, but rarely do we as Christians really talk about doubt and how to handle it.

The Bible speaks of understanding in terms of its foundation. Poor understanding is based upon man's own wisdom. Good understanding is based upon the understanding that God gives us. Just like doctrine being sound and unsound. The things of God are dependable and suitable as a basis for our confidence. In Job 32:8 we find, "there is a spirit in man, and the inspiration of the Almighty giveth them understanding." We gain valuable understanding of how he works in our lives when we are in tune with God and His instruction, the better we know God the deeper our trust in Him. There is less room for doubt as we obtain deeper trust in God. A strong spirit man has the ability to reach beyond flesh and comprehend the things of the Spirit.

In the process of sanctification, we must sanctify our thoughts. It was alright for us to think like we

Day 10 Peace Like a River

thought when we were not in a relationship with God. You need to be on the appropriate level when you are in a relationship with God. You can't go up to a girl and say, "I like you and I want to spend the rest of my life with you." 'Like you?" You don't spend the rest of your life with someone that you just like. You must make that commitment in your heart and mind to a deeper relationship. Our thoughts belong to God. We have been purchased with a price, Jesus' Blood. How much more does God have to do to show His love and commitment to us before we start showing our commitment to Him? That is where we begin to find peace.

With our whole heart, mind and soul we trust Him and rely on Him to fulfill His promises. It is through this confidence that we can be like Isaiah when we do not let our faith flinch at the first sight of trouble. If we sanctify our minds and keep it focused on the Almighty Father Who is in heaven and His immutable power, we will forever know in our hearts these words:

Romans 8:28, "And we know that
all things work together for good to them

The Sanctification Walk

that love God, to them who are the called according to his purpose."

Isaiah 54:17, "No weapon that is formed against thee shall prosper; and every tongue that shall rise against thee in judgment thou shalt condemn. This is the heritage of the servants of the LORD, and their righteousness is of me, saith the LORD." [Please memorize this entire scripture. It is infinitely more powerful in its complete form.]

2 Corinthians 10:3-5, "For though we walk in the flesh, we do not war after the flesh: (For the weapons of our warfare are not carnal, but mighty through God to the pulling down of strong holds;) Casting down imaginations, and every high thing that exalteth itself against the knowledge of God, and bringing into captivity every thought to the obedience of Christ;"

2 Chronicles 20:15, "And he said , Hearken ye, all Judah, and ye inhabitants

Day 10 Peace Like a River

of Jerusalem, and thou king Jehoshaphat, Thus saith the LORD unto you, Be not afraid nor dismayed by reason of this great multitude; for the battle is not yours, but God's."

Psalm 46:1, "God is our refuge and strength, a very present help in trouble."

1 Corinthians 7:23, "ye are bought with a price; be ye not servants of men."

Romans 8:37, "Nay, in all these things we are more than conquerors through him that loved us."

1 Peter 2:9, "But ye are a chosen generation, a royal priesthood, an holy nation, a peculiar people; that ye should shew forth the praises of him who hath called you out of darkness into his marvelous light."

Do you see how the Word of God encourages us and removes doubt from our minds? Doubt in ourselves, the promises of God or any other doubt that gets in the way of our blessings and the peace that has been promised, given, to us. The peace that God gives us that surpasses all understanding is in understanding His Word. In the Word we find the comforting Voice of the Lord. He is constantly speaking to us in our spirit and through His Word. Never in my life did I become more attuned to the will of the Lord and thereby confident in all that God had in store for me than when I got super hungry for His Word.

    The next time that you are going through, stop and pray asking God to calm your fears and remember His promises to you. No matter what you may be going through, look on it all as a test of your faith and an opportunity to give God place in your life as the head. Stay out of your own way and let God do His will. If you have an understanding through God you can relax and know He can and will handle it. He can help you to get a handle on your boss's endless tasks. God can help you to be the husband, wife, father, mother, brother, sister… whatever you are to be. Whatever you do follow this simple rule: "Lean not to your own understanding, trust in the Lord with all your heart. Acknowledge him in all your ways and he shall direct your path." Proverbs 3:5-6. Then you will have

Day 10 Peace Like a River

perfect peace. You will still have challenges and trials. But you can have perfect peace in Jesus Christ.

OUR PRAYER:

God grant me the serenity to accept the things I cannot change; courage to change the things I can; and wisdom to know the difference.[1] In doing so Lord strengthen my faith so that I can have unwavering confidence in Your awesome power in my life over all that I must go through. Help me to plan my time effectively. Help me to set my priorities with You in mind first. Help me to exercise patience, compassion and courage when I am dealing with my family.

Lord I need your help to stand firm on Your principles and remain focused on You. Help me to hide Your Word in my heart so that I may recall it in times of trouble. Let Your Word be a lamp unto my feet and a light unto my path that I may walk in accordance with my calling. Order my steps, Father, as I present myself so that You can make me righteous in Your sight.

---

[1] Serenity Prayer

The Sanctification Walk

Then Lord give me the strength and resolve to complete this Sanctification Walk. I press toward You, Lord, to become what You want me to be first to Your pleasure and as a testimony before men of Your glory. This is my prayer, AMEN.

Day 11

In Whose Kingdom Do You Fit?

I have often found it interesting to read stories of people invited to attend functions hosted by high-ranking government officials... royalty even. They would receive the honor of their invitation based upon some great accomplishment or an act that brings pride in their home country. I keep a keen eye out for the evidence of their state of mind when I see the photographs or video. Are they comfortable or uncomfortable in the presence of their host? Do they fit into the surroundings or is it apparent that the fit is just not there?

The Sanctification Walk

At this critical time of separating ourselves from things that are not of God it is appropriate to discuss this very sensitive matter. If we were raised with certain values, we are slow to offend our hosts: Certainly speak when spoken to. Go where you are given access to go. Wait for someone to direct you to a seat at the table. What attire should I wear? These are important lessons on how to be humble in the presence of those whose position commands respect. To what degree do you yield to the customs and rituals of your host? There is a saying, "When in Rome, do as the Romans do." My mom and Dad would use that to get me started in the right direction. However, the values that I was taught tell me to do as the Romans do until it offends my moral senses or personal values. I was taught not to honor any man above God. I generally have a tremendous amount of respect for those who are appointed over me. I watch them carefully and do what they ask me to do. When they step over that line we just established, I am quick to explain my position and appeal to their sense of decency to relieve me of anything that is against my principles. I must admit, that takes a lot of courage and it is not always easy.

In the Book of Daniel chapter 1 verses 3-14, we find a story unfolding where Judah had been invaded.

Day 11 In Whose Kingdom Do You Fit?

Their captor, King Nebuchadnezzar of Babylon sought out the finest of the young men of Judah. In that group were four young men named, Daniel, Hananiah, Mischael, and Azariah. Nebuchadnezzar's plan was to indoctrinate these young men into his kingdom's leadership. In doing so he tried to introduce them to his dietary plan, clothes, customs and all that the king felt they would need in order to function in his world.

Imagine for a second if you were in their place. Your country is invaded and all of your people were either killed or taken into captivity. Being put up in the palace and groomed for leadership wouldn't sound so bad, would it? Eat the king's food, wear the garments fitting for a member of the king's leadership team; what a proposition. Go to and be a part of the functions of the king's court. Nebuchadnezzar even changed their names. Daniel became Belteshazzar. The others became what you probably know them best as; Shadrach, Meshach, and Abed-Nego. I guess that would sound good to anyone except these four young men. They were raised in the way of the Lord. They loved God and were committed to the principles and values of God's Kingdom. The king's food, drink, clothes and customs were all based upon idolatry. If you have studied any of the Old Testament, you know God does

The Sanctification Walk

not want any of his children worshipping strange gods. These four Hebrew boys knew this. After all, they were chosen because they were the brightest, handsome, physically fit and most promising of the young men captured. In the eyes of some people that would be enough justification to accept the new ways of your captors. I can hear it now; I had to assimilate in order to help my fellow Hebrews. Moses is another example of one who could not escape his identity as chosen of God. Ultimately he walked away from the king's table.

Instead of allowing the king to indoctrinate them and strip them of what they had spent their entire lives learning they made a stand. Daniel spoke up and asked the captain if they could eat what they were used to. Nebuchadnezzar's assumption was that if they ate their normal diet they would not look as healthy as the rest of the young men in training. Why do people assume that when you do what God wants you to do that you will not prosper or look as good as everyone else? Well they got the permission and wouldn't you know it, they looked better than anyone else in the group that was eating the king's food. Immediately they had credibility and a good reputation. At that point, they began to affect change in the king and how he did business.

Day 11 In Whose Kingdom Do You Fit?

As we allow God to sanctify us make sure that you do not allow any lower king's customs to defile you. What do I mean by that? In our lives we will encounter much. Proverbs 18:16, "a man's gift maketh room for him, and bringeth him before great men." As God prospers you He exalts you. When this happens you will find yourself in places and speaking to people who have influence. I personally have experienced this same situation. I have had the privilege of audiences with legislators both at the State and Federal levels. I have been in the company of local politicians, business people, television personalities and musicians that are well known. These experiences were not just, "in the same room," kind of encounters. These were, "what do you think about this situation," kind of conversations. Why would they ask me my opinion? I certainly did not enter the room to engage them in any detailed conversations. I very often felt as though I had nothing to offer them. I can't imagine anything that I had done to gain their attention nor indicate that I was anyone important enough to speak to. It all happened because God had ordained it for that moment. If it is His will He will ordain it again. You are subject to that very same call. You never know when you will be given an assignment to speak on behalf of God's Kingdom to

The Sanctification Walk

people of great stature. More importantly, we all have constant opportunities to speak to many people of "normal" stature. Regardless of who you are talking to there is a danger that you will be caught up in the curtain of ego and possibly notoriety. You may be called upon frequently to speak in front of crowds of people or talk to people one on one. In all of these occasions you must always remember whose Kingdom you represent.

Do you represent the Kingdom of this world or do you represent the Kingdom of Heaven? In Ephesians 6 we find that we are Ambassadors for Christ. We represent the Kingdom of Jesus Christ. There is no ambassador for a nation that is not from that nation and is not loyal to that nation. If we can accept that frame of mind then we can begin to understand the point of this lesson today. As a citizen of the Kingdom of Jesus Christ, you live in accordance with the will of the Almighty King. You eat as He eats. You dress as He dresses. You act as He acts. You embrace and reflect the values of the Heavenly Kingdom. In accordance with the Word of God, we are not of this world and are called to not be conformed to the world but to be transformed with the renewing of our minds in Christ Jesus.

Day 11 In Whose Kingdom Do You Fit?

I encourage you to stop embracing the world view. You are not supposed to be a world-thinker. As harmless as it seems, avoid it and run toward the principles of Kingdom thinking. This bit of advice is so important that Solomon wrote it twice in Proverbs 14:12 and 16:25, "there is a way that seemeth right unto a man, but the end thereof are the ways of death." Don't be quick to believe everything you hear. Be even slower in your assessment of how it measures up to God's standard. Don't be so eager to politicize spiritual matters. Above all, do not confuse religion with Christianity. Based on its definition, religion can embrace just about any belief system that a person commits. Christianity could be one of them. Christianity is more than a religion; it is a set of life principles based upon God's Divine plan for man, through His Son, Jesus Christ. Politicizing it trivializes the power of God. Politicizing it tends to pigeonhole our lifestyle and reduce us to the fanatical special interest group status. God is more than capable of moving and influencing our government in His own way. His Spirit responds to the needs of the body of Christ. He does what He wants, when He wants, and how He wants. He is Sovereign. In the context of our walk, we must never let the world powers influence us and our view of the

Kingdom of God. If anything is to happen, it is the Kingdom of God that will influence the world as God ordains it to do so.

We must never let the world enter into the Kingdom realm. We must always show the difference between the two. This is a golden opportunity to let sanctification manifest in our lives by keeping the two separate. Everything that is Holy about you must remain Holy. Be Holy for God is Holy. There is an old hymn that says, "Take the name of Jesus ever as a shield from every snare. If temptations round you gather breath the holy name in prayer." Be encouraged and remain in the will of God. Do not turn around because the blessing is at hand. All that is behind you is what you have always had. If you want better, make sure you aren't standing where you always have.

OUR PRAYER:

Father in our pursuit of You we know that we will prosper. Prosperity manifests in many different ways Lord. We pray that our hearts be prepared to receive Your blessings and Your elevation. As Ambassadors, make us strong. Give us the Words to say to those we share the promises of the Kingdom. We also know that

Day 11 In Whose Kingdom Do You Fit?

we will be tempted to go the way of the world from time to time. We ask that You shield us and hold us in Your care. Strengthen our resolve to serve You alone. Though the world shows us their riches, we know that Yours are eternal and sure. The world offers fleeting rewards. Yours are sure and bring life.

God we are at the half way mark of this Sanctification Walk and look to You in this hour to fill us with Your Holy Spirit. We are breaking down before You so that our will is no longer important to us. Your will is what matters. Your ways are perfect. You are the Lord our God and we will walk in Your Statutes and Your judgments. We will do them as You give us the strength. Increase our faith and keep us from all temptation and evil in Jesus' Name, AMEN.

Day 12

Be Yourself, God Will Do the Rest

In the United States, people all over the country celebrate Halloween. Many traditions have been born from the celebration of Halloween. Now Halloween is not of God in any way, shape or form. That is not the point of discussing it. The reason many people enjoy Halloween is because it affords the opportunity to wear masks and take on personas that we otherwise would not.

The masks are the most obvious and outward sign of this celebration. However, it goes deeper than that. People flirt with the ability to look like, act like or take on the qualities of a character that they otherwise would not be. Some people enjoy the allure of a horror movie villain. Some people get a kick out of being a demon, (which is the biggest reason Christians should avoid this celebration). Many will dress as celebrities. Others will do the French maid thing, body builder, hooker or other naughty personas. You get my point. As a child, I was allowed to trick or treat and I went one year as a clown. My family was not able to afford a costume and I depended on my grandfather to lovingly construct my costume. He took old carpet and made my clown shoes. He cut out the upper and the lower portion of the shoes and then stapled them together. That did not work well to my dismay. Despite the challenges of a homemade costume I had a ball being something that I had always wanted to be. That was harmless enough, however, when are masks not so good for you?

One of the greatest barriers that there is to the process of becoming what God desires us to be is our perception of the certain way we should look and act. Why do we feel this way? There seems to be a perverse thought process floating around that you cannot come to God until you have reached some level of acceptability in His Eyes. Perhaps it is a misunderstanding about God's Presence not visiting on unrighteousness.

Day 12 Be Yourself, God Will Do the Rest

Well that is true. What is not true is that you must be righteous to accept the Gift of eternal Life. It is also true that we can do nothing by ourselves. Wherever we are it is the perfect place for God's glory to reach out to us and do wonderful things. Redemption is not a point of sale item. We don't have to go to the mercy store to get it. It comes to you like mail-order. Just like salvation is paid for, the benefits of the Kingdom are paid for and are benefits of Jesus' completed work on Calvary. When you ask for it it is delivered, instantly. If you have been holding out on the Sanctification Walk because you thought you weren't Holy enough to be sanctified, please know that God is waiting.

In Isaiah 55:1-2, the prophet begins writing that chapter with, "Is anyone thirsty? Come and drink – even if you have no money! Come, take your choice of wine or milk – it's all free! Why spend your money on food that does not give you strength? Why pay for food that does you no good? Listen and I will tell you where to go to get food that is good for your soul." The implication in this verse is that you do not need anything to receive what the Lord has for you and your benefit. The notion that you have to get yourself together in some fashion before God can move in your life is so far from the truth. That type of thinking gives power to Satan to keep you away from what God has for you. You will never be righteous in your own right. Romans 3:25-26 declares that God is the Giver of righteousness through Jesus Christ. All you have to do is believe in Jesus to receive righteousness. That is the only improvement that you could ever make in your own life. That is the decision to receive God's gifts. There is nothing that we need to be like. God is not expecting a picture of anything righteous. It is God Who makes you righteous and then sees only the righteousness in you as He works His grace and mercy into the twisted mess of your life. In Romans we found out that there is no one righteous. Not one person. We have all sinned and fallen short of the glory of God.

    Let's get back to why we wear masks in church. For some reason we believe people in the church have a right to judge us. If there is none that is righteous, then where is our judge? God is the judge of every opinion, creed, and act of man. He is the only One who has the authority to judge us. This belief that people can judge us gives way to the foundation of masks in the Church. We use our masks to hide many things.

Day 12 Be Yourself, God Will Do the Rest

We think that if we still smoke, we have to hide that from the people of God. Instead I offer to you that the people of God who are walking according to the will of God should be the ones helping you to overcome that addiction. Some folks are hiding the fact that they are living out of wedlock with someone. That is not in the will of God. However, why hide that issue when God can work a work in your life. For whatever reason that is happening, maybe the way that God has provided for you to escape that situation is in the Church itself. Some people think that you have to have it all together with your finances. I found that the best place to start getting your finances together is in the church. The principles of tithing and giving are awesome. All you need is to learn them. Don't run yourself in the ground financially wearing a mask. We don't want people to know that we have a child in prison, a pregnant daughter, an addict for a husband or wife. Wearing masks keeps you by yourself.

When you are cut off from the body of Christ you cannot take advantage of the power of the body. Amputate a hand and it withers. That is what happens when you are cut off from the body of Christ. You lose valuable circulation that sustains you and keeps you. God help you if you are about to be elevated in the body; Satan will plant all kinds of thoughts in your spirit that will cause you to think that you are not worthy of the elevation. Newsflash- you are not worthy of the elevation by yourself. It takes God working in you. Philippians 1:6 "Being confident of this very thing, that he which hath **begun a good work in you** will perform it until the day of Jesus Christ:" No matter where you are in your Christian walk, you are always under construction. Your life is a constant press toward perfection. Paul wrote that he forgot about the past and presses toward the prize of the High calling of Christ, which is eternal Life.

Depression and other issues are on the rise in the Church because people don't know that God cares about them as they are. Not what they think He wants to see them as. Sunday is not Halloween in the Church. Sunday is a day of worship. John 4:24 says, "God is a spirit, and they that worship him must worship him in spirit and truth." TRUTH. No masks. People of God while you are in sanctification mode ask God to help you take off the masks. Satan is a deceiver. You do not want to look like a deceiver. We worship God in all of our actions. All that we do, we should do in His Name. When we enter the house of worship and deal with the people of the Kingdom, we must

Day 12 Be Yourself, God Will Do the Rest

present ourselves honestly. This goes for preachers, musicians, deacons, missionaries, pew warmers. Whatever you are doing in the body of Christ, you should feel free to be you. A very good friend of mine put it plain how he felt about the demographics of the Church. I will share it with you. He said, "There aren't enough prostitutes, alcoholics or drug addicts in the Church." What did he mean by that? Jesus stated in Luke 5:32, "I came not to call the righteous, but sinners to repentance." We should be seeking to bring the outcasts, the people who are being stepped on and overlooked by the "Holier than thou" Church. If that is who we should be ministering to, don't you think they might need someone who has experienced life like they have to minister to them? Jeremiah 17:10, "I the Lord search the heart, I try the reins, even to give every man according to the fruit of his doing." Sanctification without masks puts us in the position to receive all the blessings that God has for us and ensures that our fruit is pleasingly good and sustainable fruit in God's eyes.

    Your pain and your shortfalls are what God has plans to use in your ministry. Your life experiences are what make you the person that you are. God has brought you from a different place than others. Your journey is what makes you unique. As Paul could forget the things that he had done, he forgot them as being accounted against him. The life he lived shaped him and was still his testimony before Christ and the world. Your testimony should be, "I used to be _____, but God delivered me and now I am a child of the King, saved, SANCTIFIED and filled with the Holy Spirit. I used to wear a mask to hide who I was because I was ashamed. Now I know that I went through my issues for the glory of God. I suffered so that others could see that God can save anybody if He saved me."

Now that you have heard this encouragement, what are you going to do? Are you prepared to allow God to take the mask off you and reveal who you really are in Him? Are you going to stop putting the layers of guilt back on every time God takes them away? Can you let Him turn your shame into a song? Can you let Him turn your pain into praise? Are you willing to let Him turn your test into a testimony, your trial to a victory? Are you ready to let God be the God of your life and fully surrender to Him and His will? If you are, then you are ready to declare, "The joy of the Lord is my strength." "His praise shall continually be in my mouth." "From whence cometh my help? My help cometh from the Lord." Take your mask off. Take

Day 12 Be Yourself, God Will Do the Rest

your mask off. In the Name of Jesus, take your mask off.

OUR PRAYER:

Lord God in heaven, I have been hiding behind my mask. It was shaped from guilt and shame. It was a lie to myself and those around me. In hiding my face, I have hidden my testimony and the story of how You have kept me. I have allowed Satan to keep me captive in my sinful past. I have not given You the glory that is due to You. Forgive me. Keep me that I do not sin against You again in this way.

I am free Lord. You said it in Your Word that he that the Son has set free is free indeed. I glory in my freedom. I will share Your love with all that I meet. You are worthy of the praise. I will praise You openly. As You work Your work in me Lord continue to sanctify me and make me Holy in Your sight. Instill in me the habits of praise, worship, prayer and study of Your Word. I want to be a servant to You, Lord. Help me in my walk to stay in Your will and under Your anointing. This is my prayer in the Name of Jesus. AMEN.

Day 13

Discernment

One thing that has become very apparent to me during this time of Sanctification is that Satan can come up with some stuff to take your focus off what you are doing. We often hear preachers speak of the spirit of discernment. What exactly does that mean? Hebrews 5:14, "But solid food is for the mature, for those who have their powers of discernment trained by constant practice to distinguish good from evil." When God calls us to reach the levels of maturity in faith and things of the Spirit, we must develop certain skills. This verse suggests that the spirit of discernment is the result of a functional connection to the Father where we learn to hear Him and listen to the direction of the

Spirit. The Spirit tells us how to distinguish good from evil.

Let me slow down just for a minute. Philippians 1:9-10 says, "And it is my prayer that your love may abound more and more, with knowledge and all discernment, so that you may approve what is excellent, and so be pure and blameless for the day of Christ." Then we find in 1 John 4:1, "Beloved, do not believe every spirit, but test the spirits to see whether they are from God, for many false prophets have gone out into the world. Merriam-Webster defines *discernment* as the quality of being able to grasp and comprehend what is obscure. If you recall I shared with you that, the best weapon that Satan has against you is the ability to make you think things are important and to draw you away from the path that God has in store for you. He wants to deceive you into believing things that are not of God are of God. You remember the great lie he told to Eve, right?

If you are on this journey, you are on it to attain spiritual maturity. Your ultimate goal is to grow to the level of spiritual ability that causes you to think first of Christ in a crisis. By now, you should have come to understand that sanctification puts you in a completely different realm than where you are accustomed. If you

Day 13 Discernment

have been paying attention, your perspective is changing. A desire to know God better has manifested in a new prayer life. A fire should be burning in your heart that can only be quenched by the knowledge of the Creator that we gain from His Word the Holy Bible. You should be at least feeling the door opening to allow freedom of worship. Out loud, adoration of the Father in heaven. You are growing up in the Lord. You find yourself pondering the deeper things of God. So if you are seeking spiritual maturity, hold on, you are about to be introduced to "Moving in the Holy Spirit 101."

The reason maturity is associated with your diet comes from what we know about the development of the digestive system. It comes from the knowledge that the more a child grows the more complex food their system can handle. Upon further consideration of solid foods, maturity plays a part due to the ability to handle the chewing and swallowing of the solid food as well. If you have a toddler, they love hot dogs. They love hamburgers. These things go well with ketchup and taste really good. Hot dogs and hamburgers do not usually make children sick. Failure to properly chew and swallow them can kill them. Therefore, we cut up the food into little pieces that can be chewed and safely swallowed. This is the dilemma for Christians. The Word of God is good for us and will not make us sick. However, taking in too much, too quickly could choke us out. Romans 10:2, "For I bear them record that they have a zeal of God, but not according to knowledge." There is something called, "knowing just enough to get you in trouble." That is why we must remember II Timothy 2:15, "Study to show thyself approved, a workman that needs not to be ashamed, rightly dividing the word of truth." (If you want a memory verse for the week, this is the one.) So for those who are being weaned off soft foods, take your time and study the Word of God so that you grow at a rate that God sets. Avoid worrying about your set pace; we don't possess the ability to determine our own pace.

As we become informed and aware of God's instructions, we can then begin to apply God's Word and practice His statutes. It is in the knowledge of God's character that we begin to establish the ability to recognize Him in His moves. Be careful, sometimes we want Him to move and we will make up the difference. Sometimes we hear something that sounds like God but not quite. Then we start to think it is Him so we use our own minds to make up the difference. In

Day 13 Discernment

short, it's not really God that we see. Satan will feed us information but can't reach the level of God's character. That is when in our hearts we are vulnerable, desiring a move from God, and we give grace points to what Satan is feeding us without considering that it is a lie. That is the first type of discernment that we should master. When we allow ourselves to want so bad that our flesh makes up the difference, if you will, we mistake a move of the enemy for God's move. The problem is that our first clue it wasn't God is when it falls apart. That should never be the case in a mature Christian. One of the most embarrassing moments in my Christian life was when I was about 22 years old. I was in broadcasting and had worked hard to develop my craft. I worked for the Department of the Army for some time and had been in commercial radio for about a year. A trusted man who my grandmother knew approached me and explained that he was a professional headhunter, (a corporate recruiter) working for a major national television network. I was inexperienced but eager to excel in my field. I felt that it was God's plan that I excel as He blessed me with a tremendous gift for talking to people. I was so excited about this opportunity that I did not consider all of the warning signs, which were many, that this was not

God's will. I even got excited and "Full of the Spirit" one Sunday and testified about how God was going to bless me. Mistake one – I never prayed about it seriously. I told God what I wanted. I never asked what His will was. Then I kept moving forward. Mistake two – everybody that is praying about your issue is not praying with or for you. There are people who are praying against you. Mistake three – I was unlearned in the true character of God. I thought I was familiar. Pride and personal desire drove me. Not the Spirit. I later found out that this man set me up so he could steal money from my grandparents who were willing to underwrite my so-called 'God appointed' career move.

It is very dangerous for us to project our will on a situation and call it God. The Bible teaches us that pride cometh before the fall. It most certainly does. We must always be in God's will in order to receive His blessings. In Luke 22:42, Jesus prayed to God and said plainly, "Father, if thou be willing, remove this cup from me. Nevertheless, not my will but thine be done." There is no protection outside of God's will. Logically speaking, how can we realize God's plan if we are not in God's will? If you are out of God's will, you are out of His plan. If Christ had stepped out of God's will, we would be lost and there would be no salvation.

Day 13 Discernment

Through the spirit of discernment, you can test the waters and distinguish between your will and God's will.

Another area that we must be able to use the spirit of discernment is when Satan throws blocks in our way. God is a good God. He will bless mightily and He will test mightily as well. In God's permissive will, He allows Satan to roam about seeking whom he may devour. The Bible gives us plenty of warning about the evil one, the prince of this world and the beast. All of these terms identify the Devil. You need to know that the Devil is a fallen angel. He was the chief musician in heaven. His very body was an instrument. With that history, he knows God. He can discern a move from God almost instantly. His job is to keep you off point and confuse you so that you cannot receive the blessings of the Lord in your life. Satan is the universe's best liar. The truth is not in him. He cannot tell the truth period. You are his favorite target. Can you see the truth when it presents itself? Better yet, can you see a lie?

This brings me to my point for today's lesson. This is day 13 of a 21-day journey. You are only a few days away from completing this journey. Satan wants to sift you right now. When you are successful, his job will be harder to sift you. You will become even more steadfast in the knowledge of the Lord. Your faith will be stronger than ever. You will speak things that be not as though they are. Your prayers will bring about much fruit. Your ministry will have much fruit. Your life will have much fruit. More importantly, it will be sustainable fruit. That means that your fruit will give life, yield seeds and produce more fruit. The mark of a mature Christian is the growth in their ministry and service to the master. Getting in the door and accepting Jesus Christ is essential to receiving salvation. The strength of your ministry will determine your reward. In Revelations 22:11-12 we find these words, "He that is unjust, let him be unjust still: and he which is filthy, let him be filthy still: and he that is righteous, let him be righteous still: and he that is holy, let him be holy still. And, behold, I come quickly; and my reward is with me, to give every man according as his work shall be."

I know that many people think they do not have a ministry. We all have a ministry. Ministry simply means service to the body of Christ and on behalf of the Kingdom of heaven. Do you remember the Ambassador lesson? Whether it is to be a silent testimony before men and women or to preach the Gospel to thousands, we all have a ministry. I knew a man who

Day 13 Discernment

has gone to be with the Lord. He had a ministry of helps. Everybody was glad if he showed up after a church dinner. He did not care who it was making and serving the dinners... just get out of his way when cleaning time came. He would be offended if anyone else cleaned. He did not feel anyone else could clean as well as he did. What a ministry; a ministry of helps. I know another person that God blessed with the ability to workout numbers and budgets. That person had a ministry to help church people with taxes, etc. He was a Certified Public Accountant. Here you are in the midst of the 21-day Sanctification Walk and God has a plan for you. He has a purpose and it is to be fulfilled, and Satan is not happy with it.

Your ability to discern what is going on around you will largely impact how you respond to Satan's attempts to pull you off focus. He will present issues that are not important. He will make you think there is conflict where there is none. He will make you doubt yourself when there is no reason to doubt. He will make you step back and say, 'this is too much for me to handle.' Have you seen it already? Do you know what I am talking about? This is where you cannot allow your will to be projected onto God's plan. If you are truly working on whether you are in God's will or not, then you will be confident in your direction and you will submit to the will of God without hesitation and not turn around. There is an old Negro spiritual that says, "Done made my vow to the Lord; And, I never will turn back. I will go, I shall go, to see what the end's gonna be." Your ability to discern God from other forces that will work on you is important. Once you know that something is not of God then you can handle it appropriately. In the movie "Good Morning Viet Nam," Robin Williams' character Adrian Chronower is an American broadcaster that is teaching an English class. He asks one of his students what they would say if someone offended him. The student indicated that he would speak softly and apologize if they had done something wrong. Chronower urged him to curse the person. The student refused. This is a good example of how to handle crisis in our Christian lives. If there is a conflict, work to resolve it immediately and offer whatever you need to offer to maintain the peace and possibly create a new friend.

As you grow, it is apparent to God and it is apparent to your enemy. Make sure that you give God the glory and hold your enemy back by not giving in to their personal agendas. Keep praying. Keep studying and keep working toward your ministry as God has

Day 13 Discernment

given it to you. Make sure that your walk reflects that of the calling you have on your life. Make sure that you reflect well upon the Kingdom and upon yourself. Don't allow yourself to be brought down by vainglory and foolishness.

OUR PRAYER:

Satan you have no power over me. All glory and honor is given to God for His magnificent works in my life. God is the Creator, the Author and the Finisher of my faith. Lord help me to understand and distinguish the difference between Your will and my will. Help me to see the difference between the truth of Your light and the lies of Satan. Only through Your Divine intercession will I ever attain to the level that You want me to be.

Lord, guard my ministry. Keep it sanctified and holy in Your sight. Help me to maintain the integrity of the ministry. Open my eyes to Your Word. Open my ears to Your instruction. Open my heart to Your direction. There is none like You, Lord and we serve only You. Guide my footsteps and I will follow You. Grant me fruit that is sustainable and holy in Jesus' Name. AMEN.

Day 14

Our Worship Reveals the Depth of Our Relationship

The song goes like this, "I worship you almighty God. There is none like you. I worship you, oh, Prince of Peace. That is all I want to do. I give you praise. For you are my righteousness. I worship you, almighty God, there is none like you." Several artists have recorded that song which captures a heart of worship. Yes a heart of worship.

    Our friends at Merriam-Webster define *worship* in the context of our lesson today as, a reverence offered a divine being or supernatural power. It also calls it, extravagant respect for or admiration or devotion for an object of esteem. There is often a misconception in the Church of what worship is. In our minds, Sunday service is reserved for the act of worship. It includes opening devotions, congregational hymns, scripture reading, prayer, more songs and a sermon. That sounds like most services that we have experienced on Sunday. That is not what God had in mind as worship.

Deuteronomy 8:19, "And it shall be, if thou do at all forget the LORD thy God, and walk after other gods, and serve them, and worship them, I testify against you this day that ye shall surely perish." God wants our full attention. Our full attention manifests in our heart. That is the seat of our desires, intimate thoughts and motivation. We have learned that Christianity is not a religion to be observed on the occasion of ritualistic gatherings. Christianity is a way of life. Christianity is a belief system based upon Jesus Christ as part of a triune God, (God the Father, God the Son, and God the Holy Spirit) it is also conformity to that system of beliefs and the practice of those beliefs. In short, it is intended to be an intimate relationship with God to the point that we recognize Him as the Almighty God and His will is the only will to which we should conform.

There are many false gods that are being worshipped out in the community today. Shopping, gam-

Day 14 Our Worship Reveals the Depth of Our Relationship

bling, fishing, hunting, television, secular music, secular artists (I won't go where some of you know I want to go), and numerous other things find their way into our lives as gods. Hebrews 12:1 talks about our faith and commitment to God helping us to avoid the sin that distracts us and causes us to lose our focus. That is why times such as the Sanctification Walk are helpful in regaining our center, spiritually.

In Texas, it is said that football is a religion. In Texas, nothing else is scheduled in conflict with high school, college or professional football games. Team and coach names are spoken in reverence. Do not speak ill of the home team. Wear the colors proudly. Missing an engagement to attend an important game, (all games are important) is perfectly acceptable. Business is conducted during football games. Neighborhood gatherings are held in conjunction with football games and practices. The support of local teams to include college teams is a community effort. In short, life in Texas appears to revolve around football. Texas is not the only place where this phenomenon occurs. From August until the Super Bowl in February pastors all over the country find themselves understanding new meaning of the term, preach in season and out of season. Preaching in football season is almost like preaching in the valley of dry bones. I prefer to not allow clocks in the sanctuary for this reason. Perhaps some members would prefer a play clock to be displayed so that kick off time could be carefully tracked by all in leadership. We are disciplined at Harvest Crusade to move in the urging of the Holy Spirit. We planned our start times to reach our community. But we are careful to never saddle God with our time line.

Some of what I am saying is not applicable to many dedicated football fans. They have found a way to enjoy football and give God His due first. It speaks to a deeper issue that we need to discuss today. Worship is the habitual practice of Godly principles in our daily lives. Worship is demonstration of our devotion to the Lord at all times. Psalm 34:1, "I will bless the Lord at all times. His praise shall continually be in my mouth." How do we bless the Lord? We bless God through our daily actions. We bless Him whenever we acknowledge Him by making sure that our conversation, decisions and relationships reflect His will. Proverbs 3:5-6 "Trust in the Lord with all your heart and lean not to your own understanding, ACKNOWLEGE HIM in all your ways and he will direct your path." That is worship: acknowledging Him in all your ways.

Day 14 Our Worship Reveals the Depth of Our Relationship

If worship is reverencing God, when is it acceptable to not reverence God? At what time each day is it acceptable to do what we want to do regardless of how God feels about it? Proverbs and Psalms are just two examples of a call for us to act in a manner that gives honor to God at all times. We honor Him by doing what He wants us to do. God has provided the standard in His Word for our conduct. In raising children, it is important to know that they act as you have taught them especially when they are not near you. God is everywhere. Sometimes we forget that fact. The mark of a good child is their behavior when the parent is not around. The mark of a good Christian is their behavior when they are not considering that He is present. To misbehave in our Christian walk is equal to misbehaving in the presence of our parents. We must understand that our worship is a constant effort every day and every moment of our life. If we have given our lives to God, then this should not be a surprise for us. This is a very important element of our lives.

The end result of the Sanctification Walk should be a clearer understanding of how our worship reflects the depth of our relationship with God. To say that I have a heart of worship means that the Word of God has been intertwined in my soul that I consider God's will before I consider my own. Job was an excellent example of this. Satan challenged God and told Him that he could make Job curse Him if he came against his body, family and his earthly possessions. God said that Satan could not touch Job's soul. Job's heart for worship was tested. God did not allow Satan to touch Job's soul because He knew that it was the Spiritual Job, not the fleshly Job, that loved Him. Wow, did you catch that one? Job's strength was in his relationship with God. The Bible tells us that our relationship with God is predicated upon Him being a Spirit, thus our worship must be in spirit and truth. So as Satan came against Job there was a time when Job acknowledged his losses, "And said, Naked came I out of my mother's womb, and naked shall I return thither: the LORD gave, and the LORD hath taken away; blessed be the name of the LORD."

Yes, worship is the Sunday experience too. The congregational gathering goes hand in hand with so much more. When I went into the ministry, I was running away from the calling. A friend suggested that I read Tommy Tenny's book, "God Chasers." In his book, there are examples of how powerful the Spirit becomes in our lives as we learn to live in worship.

Day 14 Our Worship Reveals the Depth of Our Relationship

Imagine what it would be like for the body of Christ to enter into a state of worship and remain there even through the week during work, family time, recreational time and whatever else we do. The more we remain in the worship frame of mind, the more the Holy Spirit has an opportunity to deal with us. We will develop the habit of worship. We will enjoy sanctification on the level that God wants us to reach. It is at this time that we have the best chance to enter into the Presence of God. It is in His Presence we experience the glory of God, and the anointing flows giving us strength and the power that Christ told the disciples that they would have.

Seek the direction of God on the matter of worship in your Bible Study. The Holy Spirit will reveal more of the mystery of worship to you as you grow. The unsaved will not understand this aspect of our Christian life. Therefore, you must be aware that their lack of understanding causes them to react to worship in a negative way. They do not understand and can be discouraging to you in your pursuit of God's Presence. Do not give in to the trick of the enemy as he uses those around you to pull you down. They are not even aware the Devil is using them. Just keep your focus on how you worship.

The Sanctification Walk

Worship him through your relationship with your family. Treat them like the gift that they are to you from God. Not everyone has a family. Cherish yours and live a testimony before them that declares God's place in your life. Train your children in things of the Kingdom. Make Church an essential part of their lives. Greet your workers with a cheerful heart each time you see them. Do not create, contribute to or allow confusion to exist in your work place. Submit yourself to your bosses as God instructs us to. Treat your employees fairly. Be a good neighbor. Show consideration for their property and yours so that the street looks well maintained and you can have pride in it. Care for your animals well. They are God's creatures, which were given to you to care for. Drive carefully and considerately. Be courteous to everyone you meet. Never allow your anger to consume you. Then always make sure that you pray before all major decisions. Be a good steward over your finances. In short, be the best person that you can be daily, in the Name of the Lord. These works will not get you into heaven alone. You have to be saved and confess Jesus Christ as your personal Savior. Worship is the total package. Learn to live it and you will find favor in God's sight. Once you have found favor in His sight,

Day 14 Our Worship Reveals the Depth of Our Relationship

others will find you to be acceptable in their sight as well. Worship the Lord with all of your heart. I Chronicles 16:29, "Give unto the LORD the glory due unto his name: bring an offering, and come before him: worship the LORD in the beauty of holiness."

OUR PRAYER:

This is a beautiful day that You have given us Lord. You are worthy of all possible praise, glory, honor and adoration. There are no words that can capture all of the praise that we should give to You. You have revealed Yourself to us that we might serve You well. Please cleanse us from all unrighteousness. We have sinned. Our heart's desire is to live free from sin. As You make us holy, protect us and keep us for Your purposes.

Help us to walk each day in a way that glorifies You alone. Let our speech be peaceful and encouraging. Let our actions be helpful and righteous. Let our thoughts be pure in Your sight. Let our prayers be in accordance with Your will. Let us be acceptable in Your sight as we allow You to sanctify us for Your work.

The Sanctification Walk

When the day comes for Your Son to return and claim His children, let my life have been so that I will be taken up with the hosts that wait in hope for Christ's return. You, Lord, are my strength and my Deliverer. I trust in You alone. This prayer is offered humbly to You, in Jesus' Name. AMEN.

Day 15

The Blood, God's Correction Fluid

Isaiah 9:6-7, "For unto us a child is born, unto us a son is given: and the government shall be upon his shoulder: and his name shall be called Wonderful, Counselor, The mighty God, The everlasting Father, The Prince of Peace. Of the increase of his government and peace there shall be no end, upon the throne of David, and upon his kingdom, to order it, and to establish it with judgment and with justice from henceforth even forever." The zeal of the LORD of hosts will perform this.

Why do we need to be sanctified? We need sanctification to ensure we are in place to do our assigned tasks within the Government of the Master.

God has fulfilled a promise and there is one great promise yet to be fulfilled but it will be in due season. We have discussed many things required for our personal growth. We need reminders from time to time about the reason for the personal growth.

Man was separated from God by sin. As Adam and Eve sinned against God and many were made sin; through Christ Jesus many were made righteous. Christ is the correction for all of man's failures. God gave us the ability to choose right from wrong. Then He gave us the ability to come back to Him once we realized our fallen state. According to His law, the just compensation for the act of sin is death. It is eternal separation from Him physically and spiritually for all eternity. This is not what God desired for His greatest creation. He wanted us to worship Him and to dwell with Him forever in heaven. So how would we get to that end if we were sinners?

John 1:14, "And the Word was made flesh, and dwelt among us, (and we beheld his glory, the glory as of the only begotten of the Father,) full of grace and truth." Jesus came and brought with Him the grace that we needed to be redeemed from our sins. John 3:16, "For God so loved the world that he gave his

Day 15 The Blood, God's Correction Fluid

only begotten son that whosoever believes in him should not perish but have ever lasting life."

If you started you started reading this book on December 11th today, Christmas Day we are celebrating the birth of our redemption. We are not just commemorating a simple birthday. We are remembering the day where God's grace met man at the place of his fall. He sent Jesus, Himself wrapped in flesh, to be a sacrifice for all of humanity's sin. Jesus came into the world not for condemnation but to give it life. A river of living waters flowed from Christ. In Him was the righteousness of God. We needed that righteousness. We need that righteousness. Today just as much as it was relevant when Christ was born, our salvation and ability to obtain God's grace is the greatest Gift we could ever receive. Once in a Christmas Eve service at Harvest a brother reminded everyone there was a single stocking that no one would fill. That stocking belonged to baby Jesus. We can fill that stocking with our faith and love. God wants our service. He wants our praise and our worship. We are celebrating the change of the world as Jesus changed it.

No longer are we bound by sin. No longer do we have to go through a priest to seek atonement for our sins. No longer are we under the law. We are now justified by our faith in Christ Jesus. We have found that as we believe on the Lord Jesus Christ and that God has raised Him from the dead we are saved. No longer do we have to face the judgment without the grace of God standing in our place. We are celebrating the new covenant in Jesus' blood. Christ bridged the gap between God and man that was created in the Garden of Eden. We are celebrating the birth of Jesus Christ and the birth of our renewed life. Life eternal; Life everlasting; a life as God intended it to be for us.

When you think about why you are working toward sanctification this should be in your mind as the reason. Christ came to die for you and me. Sanctification puts us on the altar of sacrifice and we die for the sake of Christ. Are you willing to die daily for the sake of Christ? What I am asking is 'are you willing to put yourself on hold for Christ and let God worry about you?' Are you willing to yield to the powerful redemption that Christ gave us? Matthew 6:33, "But seek ye first the kingdom of God, and his righteousness; and all these things shall be added unto you." When you submit yourself to God wholly, He takes care of the rest. It is amazing how God moves on our behalf without our help. What He is saying to us is, "Trust Me." In the time of trial and tribulation, trust Me.

Day 15 The Blood, God's Correction Fluid

When you have done all you can, trust Me. Before you do anything else, trust Me.

In a small town, against all odds a child was born. Christ came to us through a vessel that no flesh had ever passed. He was conceived by the Holy Spirit and not of flesh. He was Spirit wrapped in flesh for our sakes. The Bible says that every knee shall bow and every tongue confess that Jesus Christ is Lord. He is indeed Lord. Thank You God for Your Son.

OUR PRAYER:

We bless You Lord for the Gift of Your Son. We were lost and without hope. Thank You for Your mercy and grace in saving us from sin. You are awesome God in all Your majesty and splendor. We are nothing without You. Your Word declares that man at his best is vanity. We are like dust and a vapor. Yet You saw fit to give Your Son for our sins to make us whole.

We thank You for Your mercy and Your kindness toward us. This day we honor You for Who You are and what You have done in our lives. Nothing that we deserve has been given to us because You have withheld Your righteous judgment against us. Instead You have redeemed us and made us righteous in Your sight. We offer ourselves to You as a vessel empty ready to be filled. Fill us with Your love and the hope of a soon returning King. Bless us with the peace of Your Kingdom and uphold us as we prepare to serve You. This is our prayer in Jesus' Name, AMEN.

Day 16

You are Called to Action

Today is a day of meditation. Please take this day to consider what it is that God will have you to accomplish after this 21-day Sanctification Walk. Isaiah 6:8, "Also I heard the voice of the Lord, saying, whom shall I send, and who will go for us? Then said I, Here am I; send me." God does not give us an assignment without preparing us. Likewise, He does not prepare us without having an assignment in mind for us.

In the last two weeks, we have learned that sanctification means to set aside or apart for a certain purpose. We have been working on this in our lives to help us change our mindset and become more apt to surrender to the will of God. If we are sincere in submitting to His will, then we must be prepared and understand that we are offering ourselves as a living sacrifice unto God.

God is calling you. Have you heard the call? Do you know what the calling is on your life? Have you considered that you will only hear God once you quiet the flesh in you that keeps screaming to be heard? Bringing our flesh into submission allows our spirit person to communicate with the Father. We are designed for His pleasure and our mission is to please Him. It is not about us. It is about God.

Spend the day in prayer. Challenge yourself to pray at least three times today and each day from now on. Pray once in the morning in gratitude for a new day and to lead you for the day. Pray at lunchtime, thanking Him for all He has done and to lead you in the rest of your day. In the evening, utter intercessory prayer for those who have made a request for prayer and those your spirit leads you to hold up in prayer. Do not forget to give God the praise for all that He has done for you in the day.

Spend the day studying the Bible. When you pray, also ask the Lord to lead you to passages of scripture that will help you to live for Christ and to be the ambassador you are supposed to be. We discussed the benefit of studying God's Word. The Word of

Day 16 You are Called to Action

God contains God's character. The more we read the more we will find the character of God. The more we know the character of God, the more we will know about ourselves. If we study the Word, we will discover the things that He wants us to share with the world about Christ and salvation.

Spend the day in worship. Find opportunities to live a life that is pleasing to God in our speech, actions, and how we treat our fellow humans. What others do to us is not the focus of what we will be judged by. Our reactions are what will be judged. Worship is more than our Sunday experience. Worship is everything that we do that glorifies God as we live our lives each day.

We are in the home stretch now. This is the week where we make commitments to work in the will of God and to live for Him and not for us. I have every confidence that God is working a work in you that will yield sustainable fruit. As you prosper, you will be a blessing to many that you come in contact with. It is time to show the Lord that you are willing to allow Him to use you. He has invested everything that He has in you. He has given you a tremendous amount of resources. Use what you have been blessed with for the glory of God, exclusively.

The Sanctification Walk

OUR PRAYER:

Lord, we simply ask that You use us today. Help us in our prayer. Help us in our Bible Study. Help us in our praise and worship of Your awesome power. Lord You are our all and all. There is none above You. In You, there is no failure. Lord, accept our humble request to be made into what You want us to be.

Help me to hear Your instruction. Give me the courage to follow Your direction. Humble me and let me allow You to fulfill Your promises in my life. Keep me out of Your way so that as You send me I will accomplish all that You would have me to on behalf of Your Kingdom.

Bless all that are in my family, my friends and those I encounter along life's way. Bless our leaders in the community, State, Nation and the world. Keep all of our police officers, firefighters and soldiers. Keep those who shall give the sacrifice of their lives for the sake of ours. Do this Lord in the way that You find right and pure. Thank You for Your answer to our humble prayer. In Jesus' Name, AMEN.

Day 17

Committing to God's Order

With a mass of curious onlookers, surrounding Him, Jesus delivered what is known today as the Sermon on the Mount. In the verses of Matthew chapters 5 through 7, He taught with authority the principles that we must embrace for a life full of the light that He had to offer us. Today we should meditate on the proposition that we should trust God and allow Him to care for us. Discard the notion that we can even begin to care for ourselves. Matthew 6:33, "But, seek ye first the Kingdom of God and his righteousness, and all these things shall be added unto you."

Christians face a heap of challenges that come on their own and sometimes they come because we do not pay attention to what is important: the call of God.

The Sanctification Walk

This portion of the "Sermon on the Mount" dealt with the needs of people to eat, drink and have clothes. You can expand the needs list to include housing and many other things. Jesus made the point that if God takes care of all of nature, won't He take care of you? Jesus was telling us to handle first things first. We must know where the starting line is before we start running the race. Then we have to run the race to get to the finish line.

    Everything that exists has a certain order to it. Cleaning a home has just as much order to it as brain surgery. If you dust a room before you vacuum, you will find yourself dusting again. If you paint a piece of furniture before you sand it's surface, you will find yourself sanding the paint off and reapplying the paint. It is also true with things of the Spirit as we live a sanctified life. Deuteronomy 26:2, "That thou shalt take of the first of all the fruit of the earth, which thou shalt bring of thy land that the LORD thy God giveth thee, and shalt put it in a basket, and shalt go unto the place which the LORD thy God shall choose to place his name there." God wants our honor and praise up front. His promise is that He will bless us richly if we just trust Him. We don't praise Him or honor Him in order to get a reward. We praise Him and honor Him be-

Day 17 Committing to God's Order

cause He is worthy. In our obedience, God blesses us with meeting all of our needs.

In Proverbs 3:5-6, the prophet clearly states that we first trust God, don't trust ourselves and THEN He will direct our paths. There is a promise with honoring God first. God comes first. Exodus 20:3 specifically states that we are not to have any gods before God. The message is unmistakable. God wants to be first in our lives. There is no change in that protocol and no provision in His will for any other approach except the consequences of failure to give God what is due to Him.

We are so fast to choose alternative methods for resolution of our problems. Instead of seeking God's will for our situation, we have our list of back-ups. Mom's nurturing wisdom. Dad's practical approaches. Our grandparents, best friends and others take the place of God as our counselors and confidant. I used to have a T-shirt that said, "When all else fails, read the instructions." This was in conjunction with a picture of the Holy Bible. The shirt had a well-intended point to it. People usually try the world or their own wisdom before they trust in God. I found that the best approach is to read the instructions first. I have tried more than a few times to put together toys, furniture and electronics without reading the instructions. I used the picture on the box or whatever reference that I had to determine what it would look like. I envisioned which pieces were necessary for assembly. In my early attempts at this method I soon learned that there were parts left over and extra screws and bolts. I am pretty sure that the manufacturer did not send extra parts for my amusement. Something had gone terribly wrong in my process. That method only served to make me read the instructions and go back to square one.

We waste time and effort when we fail to go to God first. If we seek God first then we don't have to worry about the rest of the needs that we have. God is a rewarder of those who diligently seek Him. Hebrews 11:6 says that He will provide all of our needs. It is amazing how God goes into overdrive when we just let go and let Him do His thing. We have talked about that many times during this period of time. It has been mentioned so much because giving in to God's will is what this is about. Not our will. Do you remember Jesus in the Garden of Gethsemane? He said 'not my will but thine be done.' Personally I know that God has been and will continue to provide our every need. If He would not take care of you, He would not have brought the matter up to you in His Word. God is our

Day 17 Committing to God's Order

Provider on many levels. That would be a lesson unto itself. As an added part to today's meditation try to think of some ways that He has been a Provider for you.

So today we need to commit to putting God first. Nothing should be considered before Him. If God tells you to head in a certain direction, go. Don't worry about the needs that you have. God knows that you have needs and He will bless you beyond your imagination. God can and will make a way out of no way. I know a woman that trusted God and when she hit a financial burden, she never stopped paying her tithes. She lived in her house for a full year without paying her mortgage. She still lives in the house and is current on her payments, if not paid for by this time. This does not mean you can stop paying your bills to glorify God. If you are going to trust God, trust Him with all your heart. Do not let anything turn you around or change your mind. Make it your purpose to follow God with all of your heart, mind, body and soul. In these few days before the New Year learn to seek first the Kingdom of God.

The Sanctification Walk

OUR PRAYER:

Thank you, Lord, for Your mercies on this day. You have preserved us and kept us in Your care. Please Lord, forgive us for our sins and restore us to Your bosom. We need Your protection and provision. Help us to learn to trust You as we are being sanctified by You. We need to seek You first in all that we deal with each day.

    We give You honor and glory for Who You are in our lives. We offer ourselves to You as humbly as we know how. In the Name of Jesus, this is our prayer, AMEN.

Day 18

Fearlessly Set Apart

How are you with the issue of fear? Everybody has been afraid of something or somebody at some point in life. Fear has an interesting effect on people. Most certainly, fear repels most people from situations that they fear. When I was a child, fear worked well as a deterrent to misbehaving. Much like the fear of God keeps us in line as we make life choices. Those are examples of healthy fear. There are times when fear is unhealthy. Those times are when it paralyzes us in our tracks when we should be inspired to move forward. If fear causes us to stop functioning, it has control over us. We should never let fear control us. II Timothy 1:7, "For God has not given us the spirit of fear, but of power, of love and of a sound mind."

The Sanctification Walk

In Mark the fourth chapter those who will follow Christ learned a valuable lesson. Beginning at the 34th verse is this story: Jesus had been ministering to a multitude of people. When He finished teaching the masses, He spent time with His disciples. The Bible says that He talked plain to them. He told no parables. He did share many insights with them. After He finished, the end of the day was coming upon them. Jesus said 'let's go over to the other side.' He was referring to the other side of the Sea of Galilee. The Sea of Galilee is 680 feet below sea level and is literally a bowl in the middle of hills. The geography of that area lends to strong winds that come down either side of the sea causing violent storms to appear often without warning.

The Disciples set out with Jesus aboard their ship, as did several smaller boats. While on the sea, sure enough, a violent storm blows up and caused heavy waves to toss the boat and placed the Disciples in fear of certain destruction. As the disciples witnessed this storm they began to fear the outcome of this terrible event. Jesus, on the other hand, was asleep in the rear of the boat on a pillow. He was comfortable and getting much needed rest. In their fear the Disciples went to get Jesus and woke him up. They asked a

Day 18 Fearlessly Set Apart

telling question, "Don't You care if we all die?!" Jesus just got up, silenced the wind and waves and then asked them 'Where is your faith?'

How many times have we faced fear in the midst of following Christ? In the story, Christ says let's go over to the other side. They were doing the will of the Master at this point. They were also in the presence of the Master the whole time. He was with them. In the midst of the storm they let fear get the best of them. They lost sight of the obvious; Jesus was with them. Fear will blind you. Fear takes away your basic survival skills…IF you let it. In the eyes of the Disciples the ship was about to sink due to heavy seas and no apparent end to the storm before doom would prevail. These were experienced sailors, who had no doubt seen many storms. Life had taught them that storms should be respected and handled with care. Jesus was teaching them to have faith. Jesus lived a life of example before the Disciples and they still did not understand the principles of faith.

Our weapon against fear is faith. The Bible tells us that if we have faith the size of a mustard seed we can tell a mountain to be removed into the ocean and it will be removed. (Matthew 17:20) He also said that you can command a tree to be moved and it will be. (Luke

17:6). We have just spent 17 days talking about being sanctified and being holy. What is the point of being set a part for the purposes of God and not have faith? What can we accomplish with no faith? Nothing. We can do nothing without faith. We cannot please God and we certainly cannot accomplish anything in the spirit. Faith is the key to all that we must do. God asks us to do many things that are a part of His perfect plan. He will not ask us to do anything that we cannot accomplish. He expects us to use our faith, not fear, in all that we do.

Earlier we shared that Hebrews 11:1 says, "Now faith is the substance of things hoped for, the evidence of things not seen." You know that you must use faith to drive out fear. There is nothing more powerful than faith. Please take today to affirm in your heart that you will not let fear shake your faith. Also affirm in your heart that you will use your faith to conquer all things that stand in your way of accomplishing God's will in your life. There is a little recitation that my Bishop used to use to help us begin to feel the power of the Word we were about to hear. It was simple and has been used by other ministers with their congregations. It says in part, "This is the Word of God." It goes on to say, "I am who it says I am. I can do what it says I

Day 18 Fearlessly Set Apart

can do. I can have what it says I can have. Satan you have no power over me. I am going to tear your kingdom down in my life." This particular recitation has received a bit of criticism. Joel Osteen is the preacher that this has been most closely attributed. All of that aside, it re-establishes the place of faith in our lives by driving out fear. We must understand the promises of God and believe that He is able to fulfill them. God wants our worship and our praise. Another way that we show Him our worship and praise is to trust Him. That is what faith is, it is trusting God no matter what is going on around you at any given time.

Faith can take you through any storm in your life where fear will not even allow you to acknowledge the storm. When you commit to Christ, things will get pretty hectic and unsettled from time to time. When the storms arise in your life, trust God and don't have any fear. Imagine what the world would be if we trusted God fearlessly as we were supposed to trust Him. The power of the Holy Spirit would flow in the body Christ like nothing we have ever seen. We would all be bound in love and give strength to each other in the work of the Kingdom. The Gospel of Jesus Christ would be spread without hesitation and freely among the world. No longer would the world say that there are no Christians to spread the Word of God. The body of Christ would be found in the will of God. That is what the Bible tells of as a Church without spot or wrinkle. God wants a Church unified and anticipating the return of Jesus Christ. He wants a Church that is set apart thinking Kingdom thoughts and not worldly thoughts. The word for the day is FEARLESS. Spread the Word.

OUR PRAYER:

Father in Heaven please forgive us of all our sins. Prepare our hearts and minds for Your love and mercy. Renew our hearts and minds that we would live in faithful courage daily. Heal our eyes so that when we look at the world we see through spiritual eyes. That we could discern the truth in what we see. We bind Satan today in our lives and the lives of our family members. Lord, no storm in our lives will pull our focus off You. You alone are worthy of our trust and confidence. We commit to Your will as humbly as we know how. Take our hand, Lord, and lead us into a relationship with You. Prosper our ministry in You. Not for our glory, but Yours alone. In the Name of Jesus, AMEN.

Day 19

Live in Your Future

If you are going to ever grow to your full potential in the Lord you MUST GET RID OF THE REARVIEW MIRROR. Philippians 3:13-14, "Brethren, I count not myself to have apprehended : but this one thing I do, forgetting those things which are behind, and reaching forth unto those things which are before, I press toward the mark for the prize of the high calling of God in Christ Jesus." Paul understood the value of keeping your past in perspective. Paul looked at the past as a stepping-stone to reach his blessed future. To him his past was a testimony not a prison. Paul's past was more than most of us could even begin to handle. Let us review this for a minute. Paul's past was so sorted that God had to change his name. He was once Saul of

Tarsus, a Pharisee. Saul at the time of his conversion was sent to Damascus to persecute more Christians. Students of the Bible may recall that young Saul was a guard of the witnesses against Stephen and was there when he was stoned to death. Raised under Sanhedrin philosophy, (Gamaliel, his mentor, did not believe in the killing of the disciples) Saul is described as zealous in his pursuit of Christians to "dismantle" this "foolish" Gospel of Jesus Christ.

Christ sought Paul for His purposes despite his checkered past. Christ pursued the 'pursuer of Christians.' On the road to Damascus Christ knocked him from the beast he was riding. In essence, He stopped him cold in his tracks from going any further in his endeavors. I don't want you to miss this point. Christ took a murdering persecutor of His people and hand-picked him for ministry while he was in the midst of his evil deeds. That to me is awesome! That is so like Christ! Romans 5:8, "But God commended his love toward us, in that, while we were yet sinners, Christ died for us." While we were sinners, Christ died. It should say, while we were SINNING…Christ died for us. Therefore, it is no surprise that while Saul was in the process of looking for Christians to destroy, Christ chose him to be a minister of the Gospel. Isn't it like

Day 19 Live in Your Future

Christ to choose someone and set him or her up to be a great example of Christian life, despite their past?

The story of Paul and how he was converted and equipped for ministry is incredible at the least. He was successful at what he did for Christ. Paul was destined to become one of the most influential Apostles. Paul even experienced what many of us would experience if we had such a past and then went out to minister. Those who knew him, though his name was changed were afraid of him. Christ chose Ananias, a faithful man, to be the vessel to minister to Paul upon his conversion. Ananias was at first afraid to minister to him. However, he did what he was told in faith. (Do you remember yesterday's lesson – Faith in place of fear?) After all was said and done, Paul went on to be who God wanted him to be.

Paul's example is powerful as we reflect on those words in Philippians 3:13-14, "Forgetting those things which are behind me, reaching forth unto those things which are before, I press toward the mark for the prize of the high calling of God in Christ Jesus." Some of us would not ever be able to move beyond Paul's past. How do I know? I know because some of us can't move beyond the past that we do have. So what if you were a drug addict? So what if you were addicted to sex? So what if you were happy in a bottle waking up not knowing how you got where you were? So what if you were a thief? None of that matters when God calls you to a work. When God sanctifies you and sets you right in His sight, what right do you have to think otherwise of yourself? It is a sin and shame for us to think after God fixes us that we are not fit for His service. So is God not able to cleanse you and restore you? You say that is not what you meant by 'you are not fit'? But that is what you have said if you say that you are not worthy for God to use. Newsflash! None of us are worthy of anything that God has given to us or allowed us to do. Romans 3:10 says, "There is none righteous, no, not one." Romans 3:23, "For all have sinned and come short of the glory of God." If we apply the logic that we are too far gone for God to use us, then God could not use anyone. We have all done some messed up stuff to God in our lives.

God has a plan for you. Once more for effect, God has a plan for you. You don't think so? Why then would He even waste His time redeeming you? Why would He take the time to sacrifice His only begotten Son for you? We just discussed the argument that we are so stained with sin that God cannot use us. If that is the case then how can we justify the love of

Day 19 Live in Your Future

God in our lives to redeem us just for the sake of redeeming us? Ephesians 1:9, "Having made known unto us the mystery of his will, according to his good pleasure which he hath purposed in himself:" Our salvation, our redemption and our call are all according to His good pleasure. That means His mercy restrains His judgment and His grace restored us to a place where He wants us to be in His plan.

That is enough of a revelation to cause me to offer Him high praise from my seat right now. I am worthy in God's sight to be forgiven, called, equipped and prospered in His great plan. I am more than a conqueror. I am the chosen of God, adopted into an inheritance of the Kingdom. Despite my past, He chose me. I don't care what my family says about me. I don't care what my so-called friends say about me. I definitely don't care what my enemies say about me. They have no heaven or hell to put me. They will have to stand the judgment just as I do. There is one Creator, one Judge and one standard by which to be judged. That is God and His Word. I am only accountable to Him. When we are accountable to Him we will treat all our family right. We will take care of the business of home and work. We will be the person that people will hold in high esteem and honor. Not because we have

The Sanctification Walk

done anything, but because we have allowed God to rule over our lives and take care of us in His will and His way.

Forget the past. Keep reaching toward the things that are in front of us. Continue to press and strive for the reward in Christ that is eternal life. God has so much in store for you. He has work for you. He has blessings for you. He has adventures and friends. Everything that you need is in Him. There is no lack in the house of worship. If God provides for the fowls of the air, then how much more will He provide for His children. All of the lessons of the Sanctification Walk are coming together to this very point. God wants to use you. God wants to have a relationship with you. Not the kind of relationship that some people have been dragging you through for years. Some people want you so that they can take advantage of you and all that you have to give. God doesn't want to take anything from you. He wants to add to you. All He wants from you is your trust and the praise for which He created you. This is the greatest relationship that we will ever experience. Don't look back. Look to the future that God has in store for you. After all, it is an eternity.

Day 19 Live in Your Future

OUR PRAYER:

Father of Heaven and earth, we adore You. You are mighty and awesome in all of Your ways. You loved me when I didn't love myself. You lifted me when others would put me down. When I was lost, You did not give up on me. Instead, You sent Your Son to find me and restore me to a relationship with You. You cleaned me and placed me at Your table to feast on the righteousness of Your Kingdom.

Thank You for turning my past into a testimony. Thank You for equipping me for whatever You want me to do. Reveal Your plans in my life and set my feet on fire for You. Your Presence burns within my heart. Your love covers me and shields me from my enemies. Your mercy is forever present and Your grace sooths my soul while You continue to use me. I am Yours, Lord; take me for the work that You desire in my life. I am committed fully to You alone. In Jesus' Name, AMEN.

Day 20

Caged Birds Long to Fly

Ask yourself this question; "Am I truly free?" Do you feel like you are free? Are you free to be all that you can be in all areas? I ask this question because so many times we look at ourselves as bound and do not move because we are not aware that we can. I remember once in the 60's my mother took me to a store. The store had my curiosity because it had a lunch counter there. I loved going places with my mother and this trip was no different. Sometimes I would get a kick out of my Grandmother's reaction to my mom going off on her own. If you recall, my mother had a terminal illness and though she was mobile and independent at this point in her life, people worried about her. I don't ever remember eating at the lunch counter before. On this day, my Mom said let's eat some lunch while we are out. We sat down and she ordered our food. I asked her why we were eating at the lunch counter. Her reply meant nothing to me until I got older. She simply said, "Because we can."

Reflecting back on that experience I surmised that she was reveling in the accomplishments of some very brave freedom fighters who had suffered beatings and jail just so integration could take place. I don't know if my mother was ever turned away from that lunch counter. I do know that on that day, my mother used her freedom to do what she wanted to do, just because. In my later years, I also consider in the totality of it all she exercised a lot of freedom that day.

Despite the worries that my grandmother had about my Mom's whereabouts, she went where she wanted to go. Why did she do that? Because she could. From time to time she would not be able to walk. If you have ever seen a person in sickle cell crisis you would know that there is no other pain known to me that could bind your body up, render it useless and almost make you wish for death. After having suffered from the pain of a crisis, riding around in a Chevrolet Corvair was exciting beyond her wildest dreams. Consider it for a minute. Writhing in pain with no

Day 20 Caged Birds Long to Fly

relief in sight with your body in spasm to where you could not move a muscle versus, riding on the road to places you choose in a sports car. (Yes a Corvair was considered sporty back then.) My grandmother could not understand through her motherly concern why it was important for my mother to take her son and let him experience life as she showed it to me. Oh how I cherish those memories! Now, I appreciate them more than you will ever know.

My mother conquered her body, Jim Crow laws, and a worrisome mother of her own to get out and live life. She lived life to its fullest. When she died she told me that she had no regrets. She did what she wanted to do and on her terms. She never let her illness; the limits of her body or anyone else dictate to her what she was going to do. I think that sometimes she did things just to prove to herself that she was in charge of herself. Whatever her reasons, (She never told me) she exercised her freedom every chance she got. You had better not get in her way or she had a stern word for you. I never heard her cuss. I imagine that she would have if she had found it necessary. She lived as an example for us to learn.

Just as things like Jim Crow laws, physical abilities and parent's concern often prove to be shackles

The Sanctification Walk

about our ankles preventing us from doing the things that we would like to do, we let other things bind us spiritually. Sin being the foremost. As we get rid of the rearview mirror, we also must forge ahead by sheer determination. Tennessee Williams wrote in the play Camino Real, "Caged birds accept each other, but flight is what they long for." None of us is comfortable with bondage. It is not in our character. God did not design us to be slaves. Captivity is not for the chosen of God. John 8:36 says, "If the Son therefore shall make you free, you shall be free indeed." In our redemption, we find liberty. II Corinthians 3:17, "Now the Lord is that spirit, and where the spirit of the Lord is, there is Liberty." Knowing these things, I offer you this word of encouragement. To the children of God that are seeking His face and sanctification, you are free in the Spirit of the Father in heaven. You are free through and by the Gift of Jesus Christ. You are no longer bound by the weight of sin. You have liberty and a right to the tree of Life. Remember if God will provide for the fowls of the air, how much more then would He give to His children? Often we think about the "don't" of Christianity. The truth is when you submit to God's will there are as Mike Warnke puts it, "There are a whole lot more do's than don'ts" while

Day 20 Caged Birds Long to Fly

serving God. Think of the important freedoms that you have.

You are free to worship. According to Psalm 95:6, "Oh come, let us worship and bow down: let us kneel before the Lord our maker." Sanctification is important because in order to enter into God's Presence you must be holy. You must be set apart if you are in the will of God and spiritually fit to do so. Then you can worship God freely for who He is in your life and in the universe that He created. All of Creation will worship Him. Notice that the wind and waves obey His will. Notice that the earth yields up its fruits at His commands. Have you seen that the birds of the air reverence His Presence as a storm approaches? Worship is yours to give to God to show your love to Him. Worship the Lord with all of your heart, mind body and soul.

You are free to praise. As written in Psalm 34:1, "I will bless the Lord at all times. His praises shall continually be in my mouth." Our praises are not only good to the ear of God. Our praises speak affirmation to our soul that God is indeed in control of our provisions and protection. He is the One Who has given us our assignments even though we are not exactly what God wants us to be. His mercy and His grace have

The Sanctification Walk

restored us to a place where we are able to offer Him praises. We give Him praises of our own free will. It is only in our sanctified state that we are close to His Presence and can do so with genuine adoration for Who He is. We praise because He deserves it. We praise Him because we know Who He is.

You are free to pray. Psalm 88:2, "Let my prayer come before thee: incline thine ear unto my cry." I can't imagine what I would possibly do if God turned from us. God has promised that He will hear our every prayer. As we make sure that what we pray is in keeping with His will, He makes sure that He hears us. God allows us in our sanctification to speak to Him freely and make our petitions known to Him. I John 5:15, "And if we know that he hear us, whatsoever we ask, we know that we have the petitions that we desired of him." When we freely speak to God we can express our adoration for Him, confess our sins, thank Him and give our supplications. He wants to hear from us. He is just close enough to feel His Presence when we go to Him in prayer.

When I was young I played for the intermediate choir, (The Kids) and my friend Joey lead a song entitled, "I'm Free." This song was very simple with few words but a large message. I can celebrate my

Day 20 Caged Birds Long to Fly

spiritual freedom. I can celebrate because God has ordained it to be so. We have one more day after today for our Sanctification Walk. Speak into your spirit freedom. I am free and will live in the will of God. I am what God says I am. Galatians 5:1 "Stand fast therefore in the liberty wherewith Christ hath made us free, and be not entangled again with the yoke of bondage (Sin)."

OUR PRAYER:

Thank You, Lord, for Your love and strength You have given to me. Thank You for keeping me set apart for Your service. Thank You for Your redeeming power. Thank You for making me free. Thank You, God, for being the God that You are.

You are Holy and Almighty. You are all wise and ever present. You, Lord, are more than enough for me. You fulfill Your promises in my life. You are the God of Truth and are forever my guide. Thank You for being all that and more to me.

Now that I have sought Your face, Lord, reveal Yourself to me in my heart and in my life. I then Lord will be so careful to submit myself to Your power. I will give You headship in my life. I honor You in all

The Sanctification Walk

that I do. Keep me now for Your work, In Jesus' Name, AMEN.

Day 21

Signed, Sealed, Delivered

Ephesians 4:30, "And grieve not the Holy Spirit of God, whereby ye are sealed unto the day of redemption." How fitting to end with this thought. Using Strong's Exhaustive Concordance we find the translation of "grieve" in the Greek, *lupeo*. Lupeo means to make sorrowful. A good reference book for you to get might be Matthew Henry's Commentary, (either the Concise or Complete version). Mr. Henry summarized this passage by pointing out that Paul was giving instruction that the Church should not engage in behavior that does not bring glory to God. Thereby causing sorrow to the Holy Spirit. Strong's also tells us that the Greek for lupeo means *offend*. When our behavior offends God, we know what that means. It means sin.

Sin means separation from God. That's not the type of being set a part we are looking for. We definitely do not want to be outside of the will of God.

As we stated many times before, being outside of the will of God places us in danger of too much temptation and other tricks the enemy has to draw us away from the safety of the Kingdom of God. Through the Holy Spirit we have a covering. God covers us and keeps us, sealed, until the return of our Savior, Jesus Christ.

What exactly does it mean to be sealed? Many years ago there used to be commercials for a new product that revolutionized storage of left-over foods in your refrigerator. It was made so that it could be reused many times and would become a household name. Tupperware is a multi-billion dollar industry that has influenced our very culture. God realized that there was a need to preserve and keep His children in this world of corrupt speech and thoughts. With so much around us to distract us, we needed something to preserve our sanctification. That SOMEONE is the Holy Spirit. It is only through the Holy Spirit that we will be able to do what God requires of us. The type of conduct, speech, actions, faith and works that God

Day 21 Signed, Sealed, Delivered

expects from His children can only come from us with the assistance of the Holy Spirit.

The concept of Tupperware is simple. The container is made so that when the lid is snapped on it creates an airtight seal to prevent unwanted odors and air from entering the container. Unwanted odors would cause delicate foods to take on the flavor of stronger smelling foods in the refrigerator. The excessive air would cause foods to spoil quicker. The result was the consumer saved money and waste of effort preparing foods to replace the ones that spoiled. This same concept applies to us in our Christian lives.

The world provides so many temptations to go astray that it is more than flesh can bear. We must strive to live in the Spirit. It is in the Spirit that God works His perfect work in us. I Corinthians 10:13, "There hath no temptation taken you but such as is common to man: but God is faithful, who will not suffer you to be tempted above that ye are able ; but will with the temptation also make a way to escape, that ye may be able to bear it." Our God is greater! How awesome is that? God is not only faithful to forgive, he helps to provide a way out for us before we even sin. I told you that he really wants a relationship with you. If

The Sanctification Walk

you find yourself on the wrong side of judgment, it is you that caused it.

It is God's great gift to us that we should have the Holy Spirit seal us. He protects and keeps us for His purposes and if we yield to Him the benefits are phenomenal. So on this last day of the Sanctification Walk I leave you with this simple thought of encouragement found in a familiar hymn.

> Be not dismayed whate'er betide,
> God will take care of you;
> Beneath His wings of love abide,
> God will take care of you.
>
> Through days of toil when heart doth fail,
> God will take care of you;
> When dangers fierce your path assail,
> God will take care of you.
>
> All you may need He will provide,
> God will take care of you;
> Nothing you ask will be denied,
> God will take care of you.

Day 21 Signed, Sealed, Delivered

REFRAIN

God will take care of you,
Through every day, o'er all the way;
He will take care of you,
God will take care of you.

This Sanctification Walk does not signal the end of our work to get closer to God. That must be our daily goal. We must strive to live Holy lives before Him every day no matter what the cost. My prayer is that you will find your path and stick to it diligently. Do not faint along the way or get weary in your well doing. The very time God is about to bless you richly will be the time that Satan tries to convince you to quit or slow down. Do not do either. Keep pressing and you will find your reward from God is more than you could have ever imagined. Do not make the Spirit of God sorrowful over what you are doing. Always present yourself a living sacrifice unto God, Holy and acceptable in His sight. If you need any further help with any of the lessons we covered in this series, feel free to contact me through the church. I will be glad to get back with you. I love you. Congratulations you are now walking in sanctification!

The Sanctification Walk

MY PRAYER:

Lord, we have submitted to You and sought Your perfect will in our lives. May the work that we have done be pleasing in Your sight. We offer ourselves that You might cleanse us from all unrighteousness and reconcile us to You, daily. May we worship You, praise You and pray to You effectively without pretense or boasting. You alone Lord are the One Who deserves all honor. All who have read this book in this period of Sanctification, we pray continued blessings on their households. Prosper them according to Your perfect will in Jesus' Name.

Now the God of peace, that brought again from the dead our Lord and Savior, Jesus, that great Shepherd of the sheep, through the blood of the everlasting covenant, make you perfect in every good work to do His will, working in you that which is well-pleasing in His sight, through Jesus Christ; to Whom be glory for ever and ever, AMEN.